The Alphabetization of the Popular Mind

by IVAN ILLICH
and BARRY SANDERS

VINTAGE BOOKS

A Division of Random House, Inc.
New York

FIRST VINTAGE BOOKS EDITION, MAY 1989

The excerpt from *Beowulf* on page 75 is from *Beowulf: A Dual-Language Edition Translated with an Introduction and Commentary* by Howell D. Chickering, Jr. (Anchor, New York, 1977).

Library of Congress Cataloging-in-Publication Data

Illich, Ivan, 1926–
ABC: the alphabetization of the popular mind.
Reprint. Originally published: San Francisco:
North Point Press, 1988.
Bibliography: p.
1. Language and languages.   2. Information storage and retrieval systems.   I. Sanders, Barry.   II. Title.
[P106.I43] 1989   306′.4   88-40385
ISBN 0-679-72192-4 (pbk.)

Manufactured in the United States of America
10 9 8 7 6 5 4 3 2

EPISTOLA PRIMA.

AD RANULPHUM DE MAURIACO.

Quod charitas nunquam excidit.

Dilecto fratri R. Hugo peccator.
Charitas nunquam excidit (I Cor. XIII*)*. Audieram hoc et
sciebam quod verum erat. Nunc autem, frater charissime, experimentum accessit, et scio plane quod charitas nunquam excidit. Peregre profectus eram, et veni
ad vos in terram alienam; et quasi aliena non erat, quoniam inveni amicos ibi: sed nescio an prius fecerim, an
factus sim. Tamen inveni illic charitatem, et dilexi eam;
et non potui fastidire, quia dulcis mihi erat; et implevi
sacculum cordis mei, et dolui quod augustus inventus
est, et non valuit capere totam: tamen implevi quantum
potui. Totum implevi quod habui, sed totum capere non
valui quod inveni. Accepi ergo quantum capere potui,
et onustus pretio pretioso pondus non sensi, quoniam
sublevabat me sarcina mea. Nunc autem longo itinere
confecto, adhuc sacculum meum plenum reperio, et
non excidit quidquam ex eo, quoniam *charitas nunquam
excidit*. Illic ergo, frater charissime, inter cætera memoria tui primum inventa est, et signavi ex ea litteras
istas, cupiens te sanum esse et salvum in Domino. Tu
ergo vicem repende dilectionis, et ora pro me. Dominus
Jesus Christus tecum sit. Amen.

Contents

Preface

This book gives shape to a series of discussions that took place as we were each other's guests in Claremont and Mexico. The continuing theme in our conversations was medieval paleography. From our discussion of the impact of the written word on the mind of the laity in the late twelfth century, we strayed to speculations on two late-twentieth-century issues: the impact of literacy campaigns on the increasing number of people who remain functionally illiterate; and the impact that communication theory has had on our colleagues' perceptions of reality, turning the English language into no more than a code. Our efforts to understand the effect that parchment and seal, ink and pen had on worldview eight hundred years ago led us to the discovery of a paradox: literacy is threatened as much by modern education as by modern communication—and yet, adverse as the side effects of compulsory literacy have been for most of our contemporaries, literacy is still the only bulwark against the dissolution of language into "information systems."

We decided to retrace the route by which we had arrived at this paradox. We wrote for our own consolation and the pleasure we found in exchanging notes. When our notes turned into chapters, we agreed to make our reflections public. Since we have reached no conclusions and want to make no recommendations, we have only described a history that has jolted us into our new understanding. We cannot speculate about a future that, at least for the two of us, does not exist.

As students of the Middle Ages we have traveled two separate paths: one starts from Hugh of Saint Victor's discovery that the supreme form of reading consists in the "silent contemplation of the text"; the other leads from Geoffrey Chaucer and his outspoken, even overspoken Wife of Bath to Huckleberry Finn, whose words cannot be contemplated silently.

We are both "lettered," that is, creatures of the book, and *not* simply because we know how to write or decipher books. In the society that has come into existence since the Middle Ages, one can always avoid picking up a pen, but one cannot avoid being described, identified, certified, and handled— like a text. Even in reaching out to become one's own "self," one reaches out for a text.

We are prejudiced in favor of history in trying to understand when and how this society came into existence. The techniques that have constituted alphabetic writing—consonants, vowels, breaks between words, paragraphs, titles— developed historically to become what they are today. Certain constructs that cannot exist without reference to the alphabet—thought and language, lie and memory, translation, and particularly the self—developed parallel to these writing techniques.

If these categories had a historical beginning then they can also come to an end. Our keen awareness of literacy as a historic construction whose first emergence we can describe deepens our sense of responsibility to preserve it. Standing firmly on the *terra* of literacy, we can see two epistemological chasms. One of these chasms cuts us off from the domain of orality. The other, which moves like smog to engulf us, equates letters with bits of information, degrading reading and writing.

We discuss this impending degradation only at the end of this book. Uwe Poerksen examines it in detail elsewhere. He is one of five friends—three of whom are finishing their own manuscripts—whose contributions aided our work. Poerksen is a medievalist and a linguist, known for his history of vernacular language as used in science, when Latin was abandoned as the only scientific tongue. In his new book he deals with the "mathematization" of ordinary speech: what we refer to in chapter seven as *amoeba words*. The fourth friend, Majid Rahnema, left a high United Nations position to call for the redefinition of major development goals rather than the redesign of institutional or technical means. He analyzes the unwanted side effects of literacy programs, while we limit ourselves to the history of the categories out of which these programs are constructed. The fifth friend is Barbara Duden. Her subject is the sociogenesis of the modern human body. In the light of historical studies, she shows that the result of the self's possessive description (or should we say, the possessive self-description) is to make the body into a layer cake of superimposed texts, each "text" lettered by a different profession to define a separate set of needs that only that profession can meet. The body thus appears as the incarnation of "texts."

In view of this community of collaborators, the reading guide at the end of this book has a narrow scope. It leads to the starting point of our conversations: the alphabetization of the twelfth-century popular mind.

I. Words
and History

History becomes possible only when the Word turns into words. Only verbatim traditions enable the historian to reconstruct the past. Only where words that were lost can be found again does the historiographer replace the storyteller. The historian's home is on the island of writing. He furnishes its inhabitants with subject matter about the past. The past that can be seized is related to writing.

Beyond the island's shores, memories do not become words. Where no words are left behind, the historian finds no foundations for his reconstructions. In the absence of words, artifacts are silent. We have often felt frustrated, but we accept that prehistory cannot be read. No bridge can be constructed to span this chasm.

ISTORY REMAINS a strict discipline only when it stops short, in its description, of the nonverbal past. The critical historian, reading Herodotus or Homer, observes and admires the very creation of Greek words, for the word is a creature of the alphabet and has not always existed. If the historian tries to describe wordless societies, he soon becomes a natural historian, an anthropologist like Aristotle, whose *anthroplogein* can only be translated as "idle talk" or "tattle tales."

Herodotus knew how far the writ of the historiographer ran. A thousand years after the death of Polycrates, he wrote that the tyrant of Samos "was the first to set out to control the sea, apart from Minos of Knossos and possibly others who may have done so as well. Certainly Polycrates was the first of those whom we call the human race." Herodotus did not deny the existence of Minos, but for him Minos was not a human being in the literal sense. He let the architect of the labyrinth live on as the father-in-law of the Minotaur. He believed in gods and myths, but he excluded them from the domain of events that could be described historically. His ability cheerfully to place historical truth alongside the qualitatively different truth of myth stemmed from his having set limits on historiography. He did not see it as his job to decipher a core of describable truths in myth, to explain the sacrifice of Athenian boys to Minos as a tribute to please some lecherous Oriental potentate, as later Greek and Roman historians did. Like Plato, he retained the ability to see the myths as stories that spoke to the illiterate, to children, poets, and old women.

Prior to history, Plato says, there is a narrative that unfolds, not in accordance with the rules of art and knowledge, but out of divine enthusiasm and deep emotion. Corresponding to this prior time is a different truth—namely, myth. In this truly oral culture, before phonetic writing, there can be no words and therefore no text, no original, to which tradition can refer, no subject matter that can be passed on. A new rendering is never just a new version, but always a new song. Thinking itself takes wing; inseparable from speech, it is never there but always gone, like a bird in flight. The storyteller spins his threads, on and on, never repeating himself word for word. No variants can ever be established. This is often overlooked by those who engage in the "reading" of the prehistorical mind, whether their reading is literary, structuralist, or psychoanalytic. They turn Minos into a person, the Minotaur into a dream, and the Labyrinth into a symbol.

Memories of this prehistory become a historical source, a verbatim tradition, only through historiography. Only the historian, writing it down, freezes the source material for his descendants, as Flavius Josephus stresses in his *Jewish War*: "My task is to write down what I have been told, not to believe everything; and what I am saying here applies to my entire work." Only the original text gives simultaneous rise to source and history.

Every original text is the record of something heard. Some scribe of genius listened to Homer and the result was the one *Iliad*. Bernardo de Sahagun, the sixteenth-century Franciscan missionary in Mexico, and a pupil of Erasmus, took down hundreds of Aztec songs. He tried to apply the rules of textual criticism to several songs on the same theme all attributed to Prince Netzalhuacoyotl, but failed to reconstruct an original. In their deceptive similarity, each song, when written down, was not a variant but an original. Anthropologists become hunters chasing unwritten materials; tape recorders in hand, they descend on blacks, women, peasants—anyone on whose lips they sense prehistory. Folklorists sieve sagas and legends for fragments of oral phraseology. It is the task of the historian to develop the tools for recognizing which of these records are original sources, that is to say, texts that are not based on other texts, but represent the first fixing of speech. For those records are the flotsam from the oral realm that have washed up on the historiographer's shore, dicta for the first time broken down into words, sung rhythms strung in verses.

Writing is not the only technique we know of for making the flow of speech coagulate and for carrying clots of language along intact for tens or even hundreds of years. When melody, meter, and rhythm combine with a proverb, the result is often an indestructible nugget of language. The drummers of the Lokele who live in the jungle of Zaire, not far from the former Congo River, still know the sayings that fit their tom-tom rhythms. In fact they need the sayings in order to drum the rhythms. But no one now remembers what they mean—or whether they ever "said" anything.

In certain rituals practiced in the Isthmus of Panama, sequences of sounds are used, in which rhythm, melody, and articulation form a three-dimensional counterpoint. The counterpoint effectively prevents any change from creeping in, the chants acting as mummified dicta from a forgotten, prehistoric age. Legal maxims, oaths, spells, benedictions and curses, elements of genealogy, the stock epithets attaching to the name of a god, a hero, or a place, are all very often secured against corruption in this way. The utterance can also be tied to a thing. The tally stick that the Maori orator holds in front of him and to which he hitches his solemn oration, the quipu, or knotted bundle of threads that enables the Incan runner to reel off his news like a rosary, the sequence of pictures drawn on a wall, can support the unchanged repetition of sounds that might make no sense to the speaker. The caste organization of preliterate India can be understood as the social organization of a mnemonic device that enables the Brahmins to preserve the Vedas unchanged. Gestures that coalesce with the liturgical murmurs in a sacrificial ceremony fix language to body movements. Through all these techniques, nuggets of frozen speech can be carried along in an oral culture.

But it would be a grave mistake to view the alphabet primarily as an immense improvement over these mnemonic devices. Only the alphabet has the power to create "language" and "words," for the word does not emerge until it is written down. Neither the songs of the poets, nor the invocations of the priests, nor the dictates of rulers from prehistoric times are sequences of words. Their immense yet evanescent power eludes description, and those who uttered them were unable, for all their oral skill, to see their own speech as a string on which words are the beads. Prehistory knows nothing of these mono- or polysyllabic atoms of language whose semantic fields we plot with our dictionaries. What prehistory perceives as units can have only *audible* contours. The sequences of sounds between pauses that characterize speech are not words but syllables, phrases, strophes. It is to these measures of speech alone that the original *word* or Logos relates. This meaning has become secondary today, although we invoke it when we "give" or "go back on" our word, or when we "have a word" with someone. For us the "real" meaning of *word* is *grammatical building block*, before and after which our pen breaks contact with the paper. Plato's slayers, barbarians, and children still live in a prelogical, that is, a "word-less" society.

The historian misreads prehistory when he assumes that "language" can be spoken in that word-less world. In the oral beyond, there is no "content" distinct from the winged word that always rushes by before it has been fully grasped, no "subject matter" that can be conceived of, entrusted to teachers, and acquired by pupils (hence no "education," "learning," and "school"). For it is the record in phonetic writing that first carries what is heard across a chasm separating two heterogenous eras of speech. The alphabetic scribe carries what is spoken from the ever-passing moment and sets down what he has heard in the permanent space of language. Only with this act can knowledge, separate from speech, be born.

As literates, we think of speech as the use of language, and we think of this language as outliving speech, as leaving traces—if not on paper, then in our selves. Before the concept of recording sounds through the alphabet had come into being, speech could not be imagined to leave such a trail. Without a listener (who might be an angel or God), speech could not be perceived as anything but madness, because speech courts attention. And before this sound-recording through the alphabet, a listener could not be perceived as a recorder. The nod indicated that the other person had understood, not that he had recorded the message, accepted the information.

How different speech is from language is made clear by the fact that language is always neuter, while speech is always gendered. With every utterance, the speaker refers back to himself and his gender. It is always the total quality of speech that refers the listener to the speaker's gender, not the grammatical gender of the pronoun "I." (Nowhere, with the possible exception of the oasis of Hadramut, does the personal pronoun have grammatical gender.) In a culture, what sounds feminine and what sounds masculine is determined by convention, and not by the biological nature of the vocal cords. The way men and women speak contrasts in many ways: linguists, anthropologists, and sociologists recognize about two dozen criteria describing these contrasts. In no two places is their configuration the same. The gender contrast in speech is just as fundamental as the contrast in phonemes, but it has barely been remarked. At the very best, recently, linguists have examined the discrimination against women in the so-called "use" of language, which is genderless.

This gender contrast in speech is lost when it congeals as language on the page. It does not survive the jump from pure time of speech into the permanent, spatial dimension of script. To return to Herodotus: The historian's task starts "with those whom we call the human race" that script has brought into being; with men and women when they begin to speak the same language. (We have been tempted to speculate that the story of the Tower of Babel tells of this event.)

If alphabetic writing can be spoken of as bringing the human race into existence, it is only because this kind of writing is unique, as a study of the history and phenomenology of phonetic writing will reveal. Pure, mature phonetic writing, which was discovered only once, albeit in stages, is an oddity among writing systems in the same way that the loudspeaker is an oddity among trumpets. The alphabet records only sounds, and it is only through sounds that it provides meaning. The alphabet does exactly the opposite of what most hieroglyphics and ideograms and, most importantly, what Semitic letters were created to do.

In writing systems using hieroglyphics and ideograms, the reader is expected to speak; the ideogram itself is silent. The statement "1 × 1" says "once one," or "one times one," or even "multiplication table." But it can equally be read "jedan put jedan." In all these scripts the reader must find the spoken expression from recollecting what has been said before: Mayan hieroglyphics, for example, provide the clues so that the reader may speak aloud from memory. Through landmarks that are more than just pictograms, they help him find his way orally along an often-traveled path. Ideograms, too, originally point toward utterance. They presuppose that the reader is familiar with the content of ideas whose individual elements are strung in a row before him to be named. Reading thus means retelling the familiar content depicted in accordance with more or less precise rules. Even when—as in the third millennium B.C.—the individual Egyptian hieroglyph or Mesopotamian ideograph become logograms, so that from that point on they had to be named with one and only one word, the word presents itself to the reader without any indication about its sound; the ending and inflection that make it audible must be supplied by the reader.

The early part of the second millennium B.C. saw a series of faltering attempts here and there in the Middle East to bind speech more closely to writing. Convention came to dictate that a particular pictogram or ideogram, which had become a logogram, could be used as a syllable sign. The reader put aside any recognizable meaning of the word and read it into the text for its sound only. As a syllable sign it came to be placed beside the thing sign, making it easier to decipher. Reading became somewhat like solving a rebus. Nowhere, however, did a true syllabary evolve out of this custom—the Indian syllabic alphabet is of considerably more recent origin than the Greek. It is an admirable system of phonetic notation that grew out of the Greek invention.

Quite suddenly, around 1400 B.C., an entirely new kind of script made its appearance on the border between the Egyptian hieroglyphic tradition and the cuneiform of Mesopotamia. This North Semitic alphabet was the first to have signs for sounds only, and only one sign for each group of sounds. Some archaeologists have speculated on a single inventor for this alphabet, so completely does it accomplish both requirements for script from the first moment of its appearance: the universe of heard sounds—an almost infinite variety of sounds in every language, with men and women, children and dotards, singers and ragmen all sounding different—is reduced to a limited number, each of which is then labeled.

However, this Byblos alphabet whose letters stand only for sounds does not have any letters for vowels. The freely voiced qualities of breathing are not indicated, only the consonants, the harsh or soft obstacles the breath encounters. Its script does not yet transform the page into a mirror of speech, but is rather a burial ground for the skeleton of language. Being a purely phonetic notation, it differs radically from all previous scripts, but it can still be read only by someone trained for a special kind of analysis. Only a person who has developed the ability to recognize within the uninterrupted string of consonants groups of two to five elements that act as "roots" can breathe those roots into life. The roots grow into words only when the reader makes them resound according to the semantic function they ought to play in the environment in which they stand.

In a prophetic vision, Ezekiel describes the process: "The hand of the Lord carried me out . . . in the midst of a valley which was full of bones that, lo, were very dry . . . and I prophesied as I was commanded, and the bones came together: bone to bone . . . but there was as yet no breath in them . . . and the Lord said, 'Breathe upon the slain [literally: Give thy soul, *nefesh*, to them] that they may live' . . . and as I did, they stood upon their feet" (Ezek. 37:1-10). It is astounding with what audacity a clutch of pastoral tribes in Canaan claimed the invention as their own. As Exodus relates, Israel overcame

A B C

"Egypt" intellectually and emotionally with the invention of phonetic writing. The mummies in their tombs are supplanted by roots. No longer is it only priests who can promise the continuation of life after death by deciphering the hiero-glyphs. The invention of the Semitic script makes possible a new relationship to the life and death of Osiris.

From now on the written character rescues a sequence of sounds from ephemerality; and living speech is dismembered by the scribe, who as he listens to dictation ponders the speech, examines it for its inaudible roots, determines the (usually) three consonants that compose it, and engraves these into a clay tablet. The letters he has buried tell what roots have been read into the recorded utterance, and these letters can be resurrected at any time alphabetically by the reader.

Greek merchants acquired the string of Semitic conso-nants from Syrian traders on the coast of Asia Minor. They left the sequence of letters undisturbed, with their shapes rec-ognizable and their names unchanged, but they perverted the use of these letters. While for the Semite *beth* had a semantic association, because for him it means "house," for the Greek it is merely the name of a letter that stands for a sound. Four of the Semitic letters were not needed by the Greeks: To the Greek ear they stood for barbaric noises. The Greeks of the eighth century used them to indicate vowels. The consonants are now placed between vocals, the entire word now lies on the page. No more does the reader have to recognize naked bones that must be properly assembled by the eye and then fleshed out only by breathing life into them. The page has become a record of sounds.

Phonetic script could now do the opposite of what the

string of consonants had so far done. While the consonants had been used to record units of meaning that the scribe had picked from the flow of speech, the Greeks froze the flow of speech itself onto the page. The scroll had been sounded thus far through an act of interpretation of the letters; alphabetic recording that fixed sound on the page brings an utterance from the past into the present, to which the reader can listen, interpreting what he hears. The Jew searches with his eyes for inaudible roots in order to flesh them out with his breath. The Greek picks the sound from the page and searches for the invisible ideas in the sounds the letters command him to make.

The transformations brought about by Greek literacy are well symbolized by the appearance of Sybil, who replaces her older sister, the Pythia, as the model of the prophetess. Her story is told by Heraclitus, a Pythagorean who, through Cratylus, could claim Plato as a pupil. He was the first to distinguish the consonants (which he divided into the unvoiced *aphthonga* and the sonant *aphona*) from the vowels. Plutarch has conserved the passage from Heraclitus in which the Sybil makes her first appearance. In the image of the alphabet, she wrests utterance from its temporal context and turns prophecy into a literary genre: "Sybil, in her mania, makes the oracle of the god ring out a whole millennium, joyless, odorless, and unadorned. . . ." She spells out the future. For the Sybil first writes her oracle on leaves, then later on tablets. She brings stone slabs to King Tarquinas, who reigned over the Campagne, south of Rome—over Etruscan towns through which the Romans got their alphabet. No one need strain anymore to hear the ominous murmurings of the Delphic Pythia. The menacing future can now be read.

II. Memory

At the time when heaven still embraced the earth, when Uranus still lay with full-hipped Gaia, an aeon before the Olympian gods, the Titans were born and with them, memory, or Mnemosyne. In the Hymns to Hermes, she is called the Mother of the Muses. She is the earliest of the goddesses, preceding even Apollo with his lyre. Hesiod mentions her as the goddess of the first hour of the world and describes her flowing hair as she stretches out beside Zeus on his couch, there to beget the rest of her nine daughters, the Muses. It is she who adopts the son of Maya, the "shamefaced" or "awful" nymph, and thus makes him the son of two mothers. She provides Hermes with two unique gifts: a lyre and a "soul." When the god Hermes plays to the song of the Muses, its sound leads both poets and gods to Mnemosyne's wellspring of remembrance. In her clear waters float the remains of past lives, the memories that Lethe has washed from the feet of the departed, turning dead men into mere shadows. A mortal who has been blessed by the gods can approach Mnemosyne and listen to the Muses sing in their several voices what is, what was, and what will be. Under the protection of Mnemosyne, he may recollect the residues that have sunk into her bosom by drinking from her waters. When he returns from his visit to the spring—from his dream or vision—he can tell what he has drawn from this source. Philo says that by taking the place of a shadow the poet recollects the deeds that a dead man has forgotten. In this way, the world of the living constantly makes contact with the world of the dead.

HE MODERN *memory* does not derive from the older *Mnemosyne*, but from another, later Latin word, *memoria*. Like words and text, memory is a child of the alphabet. Only after it had become possible to fix the flow of speech in phonetic transcription did the idea emerge that knowledge—information—could be held in the mind as in a store. Today, we take this idea so completely for granted that it is hard for us to reconstruct an age when recollection was not conceived as a trip into the cellar to pick up stores, or a look into a ledger to verify an entry. Since the fourth century B.C., memory has been conceived as such a deposit that can be opened, searched, and used. Philosophers have disputed where this deposit is located—in the heart, the brain, the community, or perhaps in God, but in all these discussions memory has remained a bin, a wax tablet, or a book.

For turning this idea topsy-turvy, Milman Parry ranks close to Einstein, although it took much longer before the implications of Parry's achievement were grasped, since humanists, as a rule, are much more conservative than physicists. Thanks to research done in the 1930s by this young Harvard classicist and his assistant Albert Lord, it is now clear that a purely oral tradition knows no division between recollecting and doing. The pre-alphabetic bard does not, like his medieval counterpart, draw on a storehouse of memories in order to compose a poem. Rather, he dips into a grab bag of phrases and adjectives and, driven by the rhythms of the lyre, spins the yarn of a tale.

Parry's thesis, submitted to the Sorbonne in 1928, argued that the *Iliad* could only have come into being through oral recitation and in the rhythm of spoken hexameters. According to Parry's hypothesis, there are two heterogenous processes by which social continuity is preserved: the flow of pre-historic epic tales that are never repeated word for word; and history that is built on the bedrock of words. In a purely oral tradition, songs, epics, and sayings do not hover above life. That life is a delicate, complex tissue steeped in epic recollections. As soon as the stream of recollections becomes even potentially visible as a narrative, this stream clots and turns into an authority, a point of reference, a socially disembedded rule, the excrement of lived wisdom that a new kind of wise man, called the scribe, can shape.

This epistemological heterogeneity between history and prehistory only gradually gained acceptance. It contradicts the assumption made by the sciences that categories exist to describe human experience *tout court*. Parry's hypothesis stood up only because the question whether a particular text represents the direct, firsthand transcription of a preliterate tradition can be answered according to strict rules.

The new field of research Parry marked out makes it possible today to determine with certainty whether a particular text is, in the strict sense, prehistoric—whether it is the faithful record of a preliterate improvisation, or the line of a speaker who uses language or memory to compose a text. During the last fifty years Parry's pupils have applied phonologically governed linguistics to the criticism of literary works and the study of oral tradition. In the course of their research, they observed that surviving elements of oral tradition often complemented the detailed study of the linguistic peculiarities of certain major Greek texts and subsequently of epics in other languages as well. They have developed, tested, and refined a number of criteria that make it possible to distinguish oral poetry from every kind of written composition with impressive consistency. Their criteria are the best way we know to evoke the elusive activity of preliterate recollecting in the time before *scripta* of information, originals, or copies emerged.

To begin with Parry's thesis about the *Iliad*: The *Iliad* reveals a mastery in self-limitation within given patterns that cannot *be* imitated self-conscious literacy. What Eric Havelock calls the "variation within the same" has never been approximated by any poet. Only texts that exhibit five forms of self-limitation simultaneously may be regarded as genuine, firsthand written records of oral improvisation: First, in Greek epics, the hexameters are composed of standard word groups. Second, those word groups are mutually attracted to one another during oral recitation. Purely statistically, there is an increasing probability of finding the same formulae in the same section of the epic. Third, the line usually coincides with a syntactic unit: Many lines could be ended with a full stop or a comma because at least the meaning comes to an end there. Fourth, a uniform—though complicated—pattern occurs at the level of the phoneme; combinations of sounds that fall outside the pattern inevitably point to written composition rather than oral improvisation. Finally, this quantitatively verifiable self-limitation relates even to the pattern of the story as a whole: The return of the hero, for example, is always, in oral improvisation, told in the same phrases within the same culture.

According to Parry, the question of the origin of Homeric epics had remained unsolved for so long because it had been wrongly framed. Even today much Homeric research is directed toward looking for an author. Who was the parent of those twenty-seven thousand hexameters? Was he an editor of songs that he had collected from people who knew them by heart? Was he a she? Or was he a godlike poet who composed them himself? Did he write them down, or did he get someone else to do it? Or did others learn them from him, memorizing them, so that much later, after the invention of the alphabet, like a Greek Samizdat, they could be written down?

For Parry, both hypotheses—that of the editor and that of the poet—were equally untenable. Neither learning by heart nor composing were possible in prehistoric times. Before writing, there was no text that could have been internalized and later reproduced like a film script or a part in a play. Not until there was a text could there be a recitation. In Plato's day, there were already people who knew the Homeric epic by heart—in the *Ion*, Plato describes Socrates' dialogue with such a mnemonist. Xenophon also tells of such a rhapsode who knew all of Homer's work by heart and was admired for it. But that very admiration is already Classical, providing proof that the rhapsode's act of memory was regarded as an extraordinary achievement. No oral society supplies accounts of an epic poet being admired for feats of recollection. They were neither prodigies nor super-Brahmanic mnemonists.

But neither was Homer a man of letters—for the simple reason that there were no letters. The lines of the *Iliad* do not consist of a series of words. Those who sang it were driven by the rhythm of the lyre. In the twenty-seven thousand hexameters, we can find twenty-nine thousand repetitions of phrases with two or more words. Homer sang as a prehistoric rhapsode—the Greek *rhapsodein* meaning to stitch together, a linguistic connection that is shared with the *Sutras*, stitched (sutured) together. Homer's art consisted of stitching together a series of stock words and phrases.

We are so used to drawing a distinction between speaking (and the language that we speak) and thinking (and the language in which it is clothed) that we are no longer capable of composing aloud by improvisation. This difficulty did not exist for the bard: He was composing and reciting simultaneously. As easily as he handles the Greek verb in the rhythm of speech, he finds the first stock word in the poetic vocabulary that leads him on to the next one that will fit in the hexameter. Choosing the one correct verbal inflection from the limited group of forms is as easy for him as selecting the phonetically and syntactically right formula from the vast, but after all finite, group of such formulae in the poetic vocabulary of *his* time.

In making his choice, the rhapsode was not so much concerned with the actual meaning of the particular adjective selected. It is therefore a mistake to judge these epics according to the aesthetic canon of the Classical Age. Homer, in contrast with Virgil, was not only word-less, but also language-less. The singer of the *Iliad*, carried along by the beat of the hexameters, was able to locate and use the wonderfully precise nuances of the Greek verb forms and to choose from the enormous store of "winged words." No object remains from this performance. The art of Homer consisted of fluent improvisation within strictly limited means: the art of Classicism gives poetic originality free rein. That originality consists of the deliberate recasting of a given text; that is to say it was based on improving imitation—the mimesis praised by Aristotle. For Virgil, the *Aeneid* was a work of art: It was an object that he continued improving by changing a word here and there—until, on his deathbed, he wanted to burn it in frustration. The *Aeneid* allows itself to be paraphrased. In contrast, Homer can only be rendered—the word cannot be pried from the meaning.

Parry's theory remained mere speculation until he managed to observe the singing of living traditional rhapsodes. In the 1930s, he and his pupil Albert Lord traveled to Serbia, where they made the acquaintance of a number of folksingers who still had their roots in the epic traditions of the Balkans. In Turkish coffeehouses and at peasant weddings they sang all night, telling stories to the rhythms of the *gusla*. Using the complicated equipment of pre-war days, Parry recorded their epics on metal discs in order to check his theory by observation.

No *guslar* ever repeated the same epic word for word. Every performance was, as Parry expected, a fresh attiring of the old story. For many years after Parry's death, Lord continued the research. He was able to observe the process whereby a youngster became a *guslar*. First, the young man spent years listening to the master singing. While tending his herds, he practiced using the stock formulae and so gradually became familiar with the poetic vocabulary. With growing assurance he was able, accompanied by the strum of the *gusla*, to fall back more and more upon those set pieces; but only a small number of skilled bards could draw, even in their maturity, upon the full repertoire of rhythmic fragments. The deeper his active mastery of the wealth of formulae, the clearer his understanding of the content of the songs he heard. Once this faculty was fully developed, he needed only one night's listening to a song he did not know in order to be able to reproduce that song himself a week later. No one could do it on the same day: The *guslari* say that a story needs time to ferment in the bard—at least a day and a night.

Parry's theory enables us to understand that so complex a structure as the *Iliad* was sung in a single draft—without the aid of written notes, plans, or drafts. According to Lord's observations in Serbia, it is entirely possible that a single bard assembled from formulae and sang tens of thousands of verses in one outpouring. The riddle of how such work is written down is also solved, according to Lord. In Serbia, he attempted, without tape recorders, to get an accurate written record of long epics. It emerged that collaboration between a clever town clerk and a mature *guslar* produced surprisingly good results.

At the start, the bard felt annoyed and uneasy about having to pause repeatedly in his singing and rely on plucking his *gusla* to keep him in time. Soon, however, the *guslar* began to enjoy this leisure and to use the additional time to utter the proper formula. And in the clerk he found a listener who allowed him to spin out his material at his own discretion until it was exhausted. The writing down of the *Iliad* could have taken place under similar circumstances, and Homer probably had the same attitude toward the text as the *guslari*: not one of them was the least bit interested in having so much as a line of the written record read back to him for checking.

The knowledge gained from this comparison of the Serbian *guslar* and Homer has proved helpful over the past fifty years in the study of cultures that have persisted beyond the reach of records. It has come to form one of the foundations of scholarly discussion of the epic in the Anglo-Saxon world and has led to entirely new insights in the study of the medieval epic.

Oral transmission of epics ceases with writing, and with it, at the dawn of history, fades the idea of memory as the goddess of immortal recollection. For the Classical poet of Greece no longer has need of recollections from a "beyond." No longer is each utterance like a piece of driftwood the speaker fished from a streamful of treasures, something cast off in the beyond that had just then washed up onto the beaches of the mind. No longer are thought and memory intertwined in every statement with no distinction between thought and speech.

When epic tradition becomes a recorded one and custom is transmogrified into written law, the poet's sources are frozen into the texts. He can follow the lines of a written text; the river that feeds its own source is remembered no more. Not one Greek city has preserved an altar dedicated to Mnemosyne. Her name became a technical term for "memory" now imagined as a page: the water of memory turns into the fluency of a writer and a reader. Fixed words on clay tablets acquire authority over the re-evocation of fluid speech.

Plato, in the early fourth century B.C., stands on the threshold between the oral and written cultures of Greece. The earliest epigraphic and iconographic indications of young boys being taught to write date from Plato's childhood. In his day, people had already been reciting Homer from the text for centuries, but the art of writing was still primarily a handicraft. From the seventh until well into the sixth century B.C., reading and writing were confined, in Greece, to very narrow circles. In the fifth century B.C., craftsmen began to acquire the art of carving or engraving letters of the alphabet. But writing was still not a part of recognized instruction: The most a person was expected to be able to write and spell was his own name. The taking of dictation and the fluent reading of written materials were not yet part of knowledge used for control and education. Until the fifth century B.C., schooling in Athens was purely oral, musical, and gymnastic. *Mousike* stood at the core of the Greek curriculum: Poems were recited and improvised, rhythmic rhetoric was practiced, pupils learned stringed and wind instruments, singing and dancing. The few pictures in which a teacher is represented with a stylus in his hand show that the alphabet now made it possible for the teacher to read out to the pupils the poems to be learned. Thus a full century before the stylus was imposed on pupils, they were able to learn the texts by heart. That is to say, they gained an understanding of a fixed text that could be listened to, and a respect for the sound of its words, long before they were required to write or read fluently.

Plato's was the time of great change from instruction in elevated, rhythmic public speech to the predominance of prose speech. What formerly could only be recited or sung, can now be pinned down, penned down. The script can be copied, one copy serving as the source for another. The scroll can freeze "materials" for a teacher. It is not the speech but the language of the past that can be made present. Plato heard the Pythagoreans and Socrates. He does not claim to have dictation from them, but he does boast about his faculty of recollection. He is not a traitor like Hippias, who disclosed the orally transmitted secret teachings of Pythagoras. He is already a writer—however anachronistic that may sound. His dialogues are literary prose. He created the model—never surpassed—of the written dialogue that imitates speech. His literary oeuvre forms a counterpart to the record of Homeric song from prehistoric times.

Plato was not Greece's first author. But he was the first uneasy man of letters. He was the first to write with the conviction of the superiority of thought unrelated to writing. He was anguished by the effect the alphabet was exerting on his pupils. Their reliance on silent, passive texts could not but narrow the stream of their remembrance, making it shallow and dull. Earlier, this mistrust of the alphabet had been reflected in Aeschylus' *Prometheus Bound*: Zeus punished Prometheus for bringing the alphabet—"the combining of letters, creative mother of the Muses' art, wherewith to hold all things in memory"—to mankind. Zeus had engendered his daughters in the pond of Mnemosyne so that they might bubble and flow, not be locked up in script.

Plato, who saw writing as a threat to the meditative search, kept coming back to the question of Mnemosyne: memory/recollection. How do we bring the past into the present? He answers the question through Diotima in the *Symposium*, after he has been extolling Eros: "To what does the word *meditation* refer if not to knowledge that is past? When we forget, knowledge escapes us. Meditation then brings us to new knowledge and gives it the appearance of still being the same."

Diotima describes the search for truth in terms that very closely parallel the process by which the Serbian *guslar* repeatedly retrieves the same material from oblivion and spins it into a new song. Plato's intellectual path, his access to truth and ideas, is an epic one. This becomes clearer when we read further in Diotima's speech: It forms part of her answer to Socrates, who wants her to teach him about the secrets of

Eros. For Diotima, "meditating" is an expression or form of creative love, which in its search for the immortal is always giving itself anew and always withdrawing. Eros longs for what is permanent, and it takes shape when we meditate on the immortal truth, on *eidos*. Only this kind of loving meditation can lead to wisdom. Plato sees this search for the springs of truth as being threatened by a polymathy based on writing.

To give form to that threat, Plato "fabricates," as Phaidros puts it, the story of Theuth, the inventor of letters. Theuth seeks to "sell" the letters to King Thamus of Thebes as a *pharmakon*, a medicine to strengthen the power of recollection and intellect of his subjects. The word *pharmakon* carries a suggestion of magic and the vegetable kingdom. It can be translated as "drug"—either a healing potion or a poison, depending on how it is used. Which of the two was meant was decided by the epithet: In some sayings *pharmakon* means "boon," in others "mischief." Theuth not only presents himself as the inventor of a new means, he also presents a new kind of end.

Thamus thanks him, but he refuses. "O skillful Theuth," he says, "being the inventor of an art is different from being the person who has to decide what advantages and disadvantages that art will bring to those who employ it. You stand before me as the father of letters. With a father's favor, you attribute to letters a fortune that they cannot possess. This facility will make souls forgetful because they will no longer school themselves to meditate. They will rely on letters. Things will be recollected from outside by means of alien symbols; they will not remember on their own. What you are offering me is a drug for recollection, not for memory. . . .

Your instruction will give them only a semblance of truth, not the truth itself. You will train ignorant know-alls, nosey know-nothings, boring wiseacres."

Thus in the Classical period memory became divided into two sorts: The natural—that which was born simultaneously with thought—and the artificial—that which could be improved, through precise techniques, or devices, and exercises. The Classical teacher of rhetoric still viewed recollection as the result of a journey, but not to the shore of a river to pick up a piece of driftwood that Plato called "similar" to another piece that had been lost beyond recall. The trip now led to a storage room, as Aristotle says, "to recover knowledge through previous sensations *held* in one's memory."

Each of the three primary works of rhetoric (the anonymous *Rhetorica Ad Herennium* [82–81 B.C.], on which later Western traditions of memory training were based and which was attributed to Tullius; Cicero's *De Oratore* [55 B.C.]; and Quintillian's *Instituto oratoria* [first century A.D.]) describes essentially the same mnemonic technique. A person tries to imprint on his memory the interior of a building, preferably a spacious one, visualizing each location—stores, attics, stairs, fore- and antechambers—complete with accessories, such as furniture, paintings, and sculpture. The person then equates the ideas to be remembered with certain images (*imagines agentes*); Quintillian uses the example of an anchor and weapon, perhaps to signify ships and war. These *imagines agentes* are mentally placed into various *loci* within the building. When the person wishes to "recollect" certain facts, he merely revisits these pre-designated places in the building, and gathers them up once again.

The construction of a memory palace met the needs of the

rhetorical arts. To deliver a convincing speech, the speaker must remember it in a planned order; and to prepare for arguments, he must remember points that he has previously connected. (The idea of a planned order would have been, of course, alien to the epic poet, the story unfolding as inevitably as each note followed the next on his musical instrument.) The "palace" of memories provides not only the recollected facts, but also the shape, essential to a well-constructed rhetorical argument.

These architectonic images are suited to the shift from the aural to the visual emphasis that a script culture, like Greece by the end of the fifth century B.C., demands. In fact, Plutarch mentions that Simonides of Ceos, who was believed to have invented the "artificial" mnemonic devices, called painting "silent poetry," equating the visual aspect of the two arts that Horace summarizes as *ut pictura poesis*. For the writers of the three Latin memory texts, memory is a signet ring leaving its impression on wax. Aristotle, in his *De Memoria et reminiscentia*, puts down the old waters of Mnemosyne using virtually the same image: "Some men in the presence of considerable stimulus cannot remember owing to disease or age, just as if a stylus or a seal were impressed on flowing water."

Martianus Capella, a contemporary of Augustine, goes even further. It is Capella who once and for all replaces the cut stone of a sealing ring with the stylus, the image impressed on the wax of memory by letters traced on an invisible tablet. The three-dimensional pictogram of Classical memory thus appears as the arrangement of logograms on the slate of the mind. Capella's *Marriage of Philology to Mercury* was read in the Middle Ages; the monastic curriculum built around the seven liberal arts has been shaped in part by Capella's fanciful summary of antique learning. He served as one of the bridges between Cicero and Alcuin, to Aquinas, over which the conception of memory as a store has reached us.

And while in antiquity this image of memory as an archive referred primarily to a device used by the rhetor, scholasticism made of memory a faculty of every soul, like will and intelligence. Thus, each soul was also burdened with a conscience—a record of its own doings that could be read and examined by clergy and laity, literate and illiterate alike. The rhetorical device provided the foundation for a new activity, confession, the verbal manifestation of a secret kept in one's own heart. And not only deeds left traces that could be admitted; past words and even past thoughts that inspired the deeds could soon be read in an examination of conscience.

III. Text

The Lindisfarne Gospel, painted and lettered around 697 A.D.,
brings into sight the watershed that separates the oral from the de-
scriptive mind. Opposite the beginning of each Gospel in the Lindisfarne Book stands a wordless ornamental page, decorated in the
style of Irish and Saxon sword handles, silver cups, and fibulae, that
balances the lettered page to the right. The initial letter of the text
appears on the ornamental page, but it also both frames and pene-
trates the strings of uncial letters on the lettered page. It looks as if
the calligraphic outpourings of one capital had the task of weaving
the texture that supports the sentences. Occasionally the interwoven
colored lines take the appearance of elongated dogs or birds, only to
dissolve again into infinitely prolonged tongues, tails, and ears. Only
the portraits of the four Evangelists rise from this painted warp and
written woof: not symbols but strong individuals shown in the style
of late antique coins rendered in sharp, northern lines.

In the Book of Kells, written one hundred years later, it is easier
to speak separately of its lettering and drawings. The form of the
letters reveals its date: no longer roman capitals and not yet medieval
minuscules. Historians are still in disagreement about the place at
which it was written and the origin of the stylistic elements it com-
bines. Around 1185, Geraldus Cambrensis was still impressed by
its beauty: The designs are "so deliberate and subtle, so exact and
compact, so full of knots and links, with colors so fresh and vivid,

that you might say that all this was the work of an angel and not of a man."

Art historians have talked about barbaric instincts surfacing on these "Baroque" pages, which react against the reforms attempted by Charlemagne. We should say: The book talks as if literacy had not yet settled in. It talks through the style of its meandering threads. They challenge the reader to weave the one story of Christ's life out of four tales, thereby fleshing out the "Word of God," the Gospel Truth. Seen in this way, the Book of Kells is a kind of "Homeric page" in which, at an early date in England, oral storytelling has been for a moment visibly frozen in the cadence of knot and link that punctuates the series of letters—just as the strum of the lyre punctuates the utterance of the singer. The Good News becomes visible. Like a stream of fibers that is drawn from the distaff, twisted between the fingers and turned into a yarn, so the Good News is embodied in the spinning out of a yarn, knitting up of a tale, weaving the tales into a story. The metaphors of narration are taken from yarn and spindle and loom, used by oral societies to embody and share their unspeakable perception. Even today the Navajos and Aymara women weave each tribe's cosmography into one reality with its social geography. Both in the mesas and in the Andes the seeds must be brought to the field in kerchiefs that tell the unspoken story of the spot at which they will grow. During the final years of intense oral tradition in the north of the British Islands, the pages of the Book of Kells make a wordless tale of this kind visible, even to the unlettered. But for the reader, what is on the page is not the same as what is in the book. The letters and the lines tell the same story in dissymmetric, mutually untranslatable ways. The knotted lines that occasionally spawn figures are not yet illustrations to the text, for the texture of the lettered rows has not yet arranged itself to be perceived by the eyes as a visible "text."

The idea of the "text" that is in the book could not come about without major changes in the elements that are visible on the page. By pointing to the arrangement of lines and colors on the page, the emergence of a "text" can be followed, even by a modern illiterate— one who cannot decipher the insular majuscule in which the Book of Kells is written, or who cannot understand a single sentence in Latin. The transformation of the manuscript page during the eight hundred years that precede Gutenberg illustrates the steps through which the mind of the West has come into being.

T WAS NOT until the Middle Ages that letters ushered in a new type of society. The role played by letters in the birth of this new kind of society can be studied on two levels. On one level, new ways of doing business, nourishing prayer life, and administering justice all became feasible through the written preservation of words. In the twelfth century neither the heresies nor the new orders, neither the new towns nor their universities could be understood without the new and broad spread of the word that was now not only said but read.

The second way letters changed a society—by their own symbolism getting under a culture's skin and changing social perception in terms of the written word—has been much less studied and is much more difficult to talk about. The reason for this research lacuna is probably that all the categories by which we talk about past societies have been acquired by reading. By their very nature they serve to *describe*. They are directly suited to saying things about a society in which social relations are governed by a reliance on written language. Even as poets, we are men of letters. What we call science originates from description. Absurdly, we speak of the surviving body of oral traditions as "oral literature," which literally means "oral writing." Consequently, it is very difficult to convey how society was turned inside out by the spread of writing in the Middle Ages.

In the part of Europe lying north of the Alps, between the middle of the twelfth century and the end of the thirteenth, an unprecedented change occurred in the nature of social relations: Trust, power, possession, and everyday status were henceforth functions of the alphabet. The use of documents, together with a new way of shaping the written page, turned writing, which in the Early and High Middle Ages had been extolled and honored as a mysterious embodiment of the Word of God, into a constituent element in the mediation of mundane relations.

So long as literacy was confined to minorities, as was the case until the High Middle Ages, power was exercised in the form of foreign rule. Relying on his *Calendarium*, in 1186—scarcely four years after his election—Abbot Samson, a foreigner, knew every bushel owed on every hide of St. Edmund's land. Even though the tenant knew no letters—the Abbot's means of recollection was as foreign to him as the book of the Day of Judgement—writing had left an impression on his soul as if it were a whip. He was now under the coercion of writing to pay those debts that he did not care to remember.

As literacy became more general and, by the end of the medieval period, embraced large sections of society, changes began to seep into everyone's everyday life. Without obliterating social relations based on orality in a uniform way, it engendered a growing tension between custom and legality.

In the committing of oaths to writing, we can trace the shift of trust from the validly given word to a document exerting legal force. An oath is a ceremonial giving of one's word, a spoken promise. This kind of emphatic utterance seems to occur among all peoples. An oath swears to a given word. The truth or intention of the thing sworn to is reinforced by a ritual association between word and gesture, both traditional in form. The latter invests the former with a peculiar power. Oaths are among the forms of utterance most carefully guarded against change. Their formulation in terms of rhythm, alliteration, and repetition keeps them from falling into oblivion, like unforgettable fragments of a forgotten past. Often the form of the oath was recited to the person making it—in the Germanic world with the oath stick held out. While taking the oath, the swearer laid his hand on the temple stele, on a clod of earth, or on his sword, or he raised his weapon skyward and placed a foot on a stone. "By the ship's side and the shield's rim, by the sword's edge and the horse's thigh" was how the Danes swore fealty. The swearing of an oath took place in the open air—in eighteenth-century Polish courtrooms, oaths were still sworn by an open window—in order to make the oath manifest to the gods, the spirits, or the dead. While swearing to fulfill his oath, the swearer raised his sword or raised three fingers or laid them against his beard or testicles, and in many places he sullied himself with the blood of a sacrificed animal. Women swore with different gestures than men, laying a hand on their breast or braids or belly.

A man who makes an oath pronounces a conditional curse against himself; he asks to be maimed, withered, or blinded, if he is pronouncing a falsehood or should ever break his word. He swears his own body, his limbs, his eyes, his honor, even his descendents, by putting them up as a pledge. Through the medium of co-jurors, he physically makes his whole tribe a party to his oath, involving them all in his pledge. May lightning strike them, may the devil take them, may his wife bear him a crippled child if he is lying.

For the onlookers, the unity of word and gesture has something of the effect of a sacrament. The swearing of an oath makes the word visible—not on paper, but in the living body of the person concerned. It incarnates the veracity of what he is saying. In the context of orality, truth is inseparable from veracity. The oath reveals an epiphany of this unity of form and content that captures the essence of the oral mentality.

The oath survived tenaciously in written law despite being in fundamental contradiction to the nature of the letter. Written law seeks to legitimatize itself by controlling the oath, which it does by monopolizing it. When strict laws were passed against oath taking and cursing outside the courts, the oath's function was reversed, as can be seen in medieval records.

When the splendidly bound Book of the Gospels replaced the oath-taker's own beard, the rim of his shield, or the pommel of his sword in solemnifying the oath, a new relationship began between the oath and writing: The book as object was incorporated into the gestures accompanying the self-curse, while its contents, oddly enough, remained outside the wording of the oath. What makes this even more peculiar is the fact that Matthew 5:33-36 contains an unqualified prohibition of oaths of any kind: "You have learned that they were told, 'Do not break your oath,' and 'Oaths sworn to the Lord must be kept.' But what I tell you is this: You are not to swear at all—not by heaven, for it is God's throne, nor by earth, for it is His footstool, nor by Jerusalem, for it is the city of the

great King, nor by your own head. . . ." In spite of this un-
ambiguous passage in the Sermon on the Mount, Emperor
Justinian's legal reforms require those taking oaths to place
a hand on the Gospels.

This innovation is all the more instructive for the fact that
the reform by the Christian Byzantine Emperor, in 528 A.D.,
first elevated the oath in Roman law to the status of a general
obligation in legal proceedings. Missionaries then introduced
the oath with the Gospels to traditional courts north of the
Alps. Litigants in these courts were no longer to swear on a
ring that had been dipped in the blood of a sacrificial animal,
but on the cross, on relics, on the altar—and on the Gospels.
This was required by the Lex Ribuaria in 803. The Church
assumed the divine task of punishing the breaking of an oath.

The use of the book in the pantomime of legal gesture soon
led to the form of words used in the ceremony being committed to writing. The traditional cursing of oneself was replaced by an ingenious formula. In England it had become so
complicated and strange that the plaintiff preferred to grasp
the red-hot iron of ordeal rather than take the Gospels in his
hand. He knew that he could never repeat the formula without
making a mistake, and that would have been tantamount to a
breach of oath.

Not only the oath but also broad areas of everyday life that
had previously been governed by oral usage were made subject to a new formal and legal kind of literacy in the Middle
Ages. A large section of the population discovered in this period that, before objects could be owned or rights made use
of, they first had to be described, and held on a parchment:
trust shifted from the given word to a sealed document.

Objects could now properly be "held" rather than possessed. The world that the theologians had represented as a book, the Book of God that man must decipher, now through the document became an object that only description could appropriate. Thousands of topographical descriptions have come down to us from this period; boundaries became effective through these descriptions: "From the old oak tree along the stream as far as the big rock and thence in a straight line uphill to the wall. . . . " This appropriative description of reality began as a jurisprudential method before it became the foundation of natural sciences.

M.T. Clanchy, on whose work we shall draw, estimates that in twelfth-century England, not more than thirty thousand charters were drawn up. In the period 1250–1350, by contrast, several million were made out in England alone—that amounts to almost five charters for each piece of describable property. Accompanying this change, writing materials increased ten- to twenty-fold in this period. The consumption of sealing wax at the royal chancery in England rose from three pounds per week in 1226, to thirteen pounds in 1256, and thirty-one pounds just ten years later in 1266. More sheep had to give up their skins as parchments for the purposes of documentation during a royal court hearing. At the beginning of the thirteenth century, it was a matter of a few dozen. For a perfectly ordinary session in Suffolk in 1283, over five hundred were skinned.

Not only the charters but also the *breve*, or brief, and the "letter" came into more common use. This can be shown by the number of such royal mandates that have come down to us from the period 1080–1180: For French kings this rose from 3 to 60; for English kings, from 25 to 115; and for popes, from 22 to 180. After 1180, the growth rate skyrocketed.

From the reign of Innocent III (1198–1215), 280 survive; from that of Innocent IV (1243–54), 730; and from that of Boniface VIII (1294–1303), 50,000.

In the twelfth century, the chancery was an exclusive attribute of the sovereign. Chancellor Becket already had an army of clerks to do his paperwork: Sixteen different hands can be distinguished under his control in the years 1155–1158. But then, beginning around 1200, individual bishops and princes began to join in. They could not manage any longer occasionally summoning a curate to read to them or to write for them. By 1350 the chancery was an essential element of spiritual and temporal dominion. Writing rooms multiplied even faster than mills, first widely used at this time for pumping, crushing, hammering, and darning. In the eleventh century, pieces of writing and articles of jewelry had been preserved in reliquaries as treasures next to the bones of saints. The overflow of charters, briefs, and copies thereof flushed these treasures out of their arks. What had been an heirloom was now an instrument of proof.

Into the twelfth century, the letter was often the visible indication of the importance, the weight, that attached to the news brought by the messenger. The letter became necessary only when the messenger was unworthy of the sender: When Jaufre Rubel sent a song to his lady by his own court jester, he insisted that he sing without handing her the piece of parchment. Some twelfth-century love letters are works of scholarship or works of art that refer the reader to the messenger for interpretation.

Only slowly did the missive become a memorial of a promise that the sender places in the hand of the recipient. In 1142, Heloise's letter to Abbot Peter the Venerable clearly implies this. Abelard, her husband and castrated lover, had died as an exemplary monk in Cluny. Abbot Peter had him cooked and boned and the dry remains conveyed to the Paraclete for burial in a grave where Heloise could later join him. With the remains he sent Heloise a deeply moving letter of admiration for Abelard, and of praise for her. But she was not content. In her answer she requests from Abbot Peter a written promise that the monks at Cluny will forever honor and remember her dead husband. In addition to Peter's note having the nature of a sign, she requests an instrument on which the future demands of the recipient are to be based.

This becomes quite clear in testaments. A person's last will is no longer expressed through the presentation of a symbol, for example, a handful of heritable soil, a key, or a sword. A sealed document now takes the place of the thing. The inheritance is no longer determined by the witnesses of a person's last words spoken from his deathbed, but by a charter. The document itself becomes an instrument of witness.

"In witness whereof" signified an action, a gesture accompanied by words, an oath, coupled with the transmission of an object, by which sovereignty, or title, or rights of property were ceded. Leaving a dagger or a goblet might serve as a sign for the bequest of a piece of land. Later, the object sometimes bore an inscription. On the pommel of a whip in the possession of St. Albans Abbey we find the words to the effect that "this is a gift of four mares by Gilbert of Novo Castello." In this way the word, in conjunction with a tangible sign, was "witness." In the thirteenth century, word and sign collapsed into a written statement. In an initial step it was a paper record of a past event. In a second step, the preparing of the parchment itself became the event described. Lawyers by 1180 insist that the instrument of witness should record a past agreement, *in perfectum*. One's word, through the signature, constituted assent to a written text.

Good faith being committed to a written document in this way made it important for the person issuing it and the recipient to have a copy of it. Otherwise, the scriptorium of the monastery that the sovereign had endowed with a gift could turn out unlimited numbers of instruments, attributed to his predecessors, which the sovereign's chancellor would have to honor. Nowadays if one attempted to acquire rights by producing written confirmation of fabricated promises, it would be understood as forgery. This was not so in the eleventh and twelfth centuries; the legal way of conferring rights substantiated by instruments of witness—not just incidentally supported by a memorial—was too new a concept. "Documentation," and the necessity for the issuer to keep a precise copy of the instrument, represent technical discoveries of the late twelfth century. The regest, the catalogue, the copy, the seal, the date, and the signature, are decisive elements of the new technique.

The making of regests, which are registers of the dictates of the sovereign, was already known to Roman lawyers. One or two popes had practiced it in the fourth century. From Innocent III on, it was the rule in the Roman Curia, but it was not until the fourteenth century that it became established in the chancellory of the Holy Roman Empire. Cataloguing techniques lagged behind the manufacture of copy instruments until well into the fifteenth century. Monastery libraries in the High Middle Ages had monks who remembered where to find manuscripts but as yet had no catalogues. Monks in the older monasteries in particular knew better than their patrons what the latter held in their archives and thus were able to produce forgeries easily.

The first known *scrutinium* of a monastery library, a catalogue intended to serve as the annual inventory, dates from around 1170. With this invention, the book became dislocated from the sacristy. The book repository became an archive, pure and simple—a library. A report by a Dominican in 1260 tells of books being set out on shelves so the brothers might consult them *in promptu*—in readiness. It became important to verify the quotation from a theological authority, much as the described border of a forest had to be authenticated by reference to written evidence. In the thirteenth century, the making of catalogues of books owned and the making of regests, or registers, or charters granted proceeded in parallel.

There was a fundamental difference, however, between making a copy of a book in a monastery scriptorium and making a copy of a charter in a chancellory. The original of the book stayed in the monastery, while the original of the charter left the chancellory. The chancellor was responsible for the copy that remained *iden*—that is, the same as, *identical* to the original.

Making exact copies called not only for twice as much writing work but also for correction of the copy. In 1283, Cambridge established the first *beneficium* for a paid corrector. His job was to check documents according to form (*ratio*), legibility (*lettera*), word order (*dictio*), and spelling (*sillibo*). Two documents being identical thus became a new criterion of their legal validity. Two hundred years before Gutenberg, archives gave rise to the intellectual prototype of printed matter: an original (that might not exist anymore) from which a number of identical copies had been produced and written. In fourteenth-century depictions of a law-court clerk, the corrector is often shown looking over the shoulder of a secretary and a copyist to verify and certify the identity of two documents. The issue of a notary's certificate attesting to the identity of two texts became a flourishing business. Even people now required identification. As early as 1248, Goliards in Burgundy were obliged to carry written credentials: the first step toward the "identification" of a person as an "individual."

To keep the individual charter identifiable forever, it must not only be vouched for by a copy, but also firmly placed in space and in a new kind of time. The place of issuance is already indicated on most eleventh-century documents. When the documents indicated time, this was usually related to events significant enough to stick in the memory of witnesses to the proceedings described. The document was drawn up on the Feast of St. Severinus, on a market day, at the vigil of a wedding, on the anniversary of the foundation of a monastery, or perhaps on the occasion of a visitation by the sovereign. It was not until some time in the thirteenth century that notaries ventured to place so trivial a proceeding as a change of ownership of a piece of farmland in direct relation to the birth of the Lord and thus to the course of the history of human salvation. Through this method, the history of salvation was chartered as the history of the world.

As a result of this dating, time through the text became something new: no more the subjective experience of a relative distance in the course of the world or the pilgrimage of the writer, but an axis for absolute reference on which charters could be nailed like labels. By the end of the fourteenth century, the date on a charter could even be tied to the mechanical tower-clock. "Circiter nona pulsatione horologi," announced the contract, and at nine o'clock the document was signed. Memory grew a new dimension. Memories could now be shelved behind each other, not according to their importance or affinity, but according to the date from which they issue. And in the Dance of Death, the skeleton man begins to appear with an hourglass: By the fifteenth century, he insists that time is scarce.

The signature also changed its function in this transition from the description of an event to the production of an instrument that was essential to the event, because the signature helped render individual will "visible," and thus helped fix it in a universal grid. The swearer's resounding name no longer leaves an impression.

In the twelfth century, documents still spoke aloud: "The letters are symbols of things and have such power that they bring the speech of the person present to our ear without his voice." So said John of Salisbury (d. 1180), sometime secretary to Thomas à Becket, a sarcastic and elegant writer who with this definition harks back to Isidore of Seville, whose letters "indicate figures speaking with sounds." Until it had been promulgated (by a herald, "heard"), a legislative act had no legal validity. The written copy was as yet no more than a record of that oral promulgation.

So long as the document was conceived only as a reminder of something proclaimed, its sealing with a signet ring or a signature was an emphatic confirmation of the oral event it described; but not yet its authentication. Because he was not concerned with authentication, the same person arbitrarily used a different signature each time. This changed in the thirteenth and fourteenth centuries when documents became legally effective instruments. Courts concerned themselves with the question of authenticity. *Vellum* (calfskin) was replaced by *membranum* (sheepskin), which was thinner, did not easily permit erasures, and prevented forgeries. Signed documents were now required to stand as a guarantee.

The old Frankish *wera*, the old French *warandir*, "guarantor," slowly turned into a written warranty that drew its force from being signed. The seal became a mark of the power of writing. Even a man who could not himself write was empowered by the seal to take legally valid action on his own behalf by issuing documents. If his word was invalid, he could speak through the document, thus exercising his power by taking legal action. In the thirteenth century, even villeins, free peasants, occasionally carried their own seals and so could obtain a description of their property drawn up by a notary. In the twelfth century, the seal was still regarded by its owner much like any other object—a dagger, a chalice, or a whip. Like the St. Albans' whip pommel that stood for four mares, the sealed wax was the object through which a piece of property might change hands. If a document was at all attached to the sealed wax, which sometimes weighed more than a pound, this parchment was mainly a further inscription on the seal, analogous to the inscription scratched on the pommel of the whip. Only slowly did the seal change from a thing (a *res*) into the substitute for a person's handwritten signature. The text itself overshadowed its material vehicle, and threw this shadow deep into the daily life of everyone who purchased, inherited, sold, or lost property. Just as in the transition from orality to literacy, language became detached from the speaker, so the text was no longer viewed as an extension of the event but assumed its own authenticity separate from the event.

Representations of the Last Judgement appear at this time in the arched spaces above many church doors that show how the book has separated from its writer. The Archangel Michael weighs the soul to establish if it may ascend into Paradise or must be cast into Hell. And, on quite a few of these reliefs, the Judge Himself holds the book, in which every deed and desire, nay every word and thought of the dead has been written down. Without ever having touched a pen or held a book, without ever having dictated a line or sealed a charter, every time he enters the church door the faithful is reminded that, even with his most secret thought, he *writes* the text of his life, by which he will be judged on that ominous day.

To write, however, at the time when the Book of Life gained prominence in Christian preaching did not yet mean to clutch a pen and draw letters on a parchment. What it meant to write can be well documented from the manner in which Bernard's scriptorium was organized. Bernard, Abbot of Clairvaux in the early twelfth century, does not write with his hand. Like Cicero, the Abbot spoke emphatically in the presence of a scribe. He spoke clearly, but slower than the Roman, because unlike the latter's slave Tiro, Bernard's amanuensis (his secretary: literally, he who lends him his hand) did not know how to take shorthand. Some of Bernard's dictations survive in two versions that textual criticism is unable to reduce to a single original. These are undoubtedly two different secretaries' notes of the same sermon of which different fair copies were made from a wax tablet. Many of the old texts were prepared by secretaries in this way from statements by their dictators.

Once a fair copy had been made of his dictation, Bernard occasionally might have had it read back to him for checking. But there was no question as yet, for him, of a correction from a manuscript.

Some half dozen technical innovations in writing had to become commonplace before the author himself could become a writer. In this period the usual method of writing, both for copying and for originals, was and remained dictation.

In the Republican period of ancient Rome, to dictate meant to speak in the elevated, rhythmic manner of the *ductus*; *scribere* meant the physical act of writing as well as composing. In the Middle Ages the frontier between the two meanings was located quite differently. *Dictare* referred to the act of creating a text, and *scribere* simply to the work done with writing materials. It was suggested occasionally that, when he was alone in his cell, a monk could dictate. Up until the twelfth century, the *ars dictaminis* was the art of reading and composing rather than that of reading and writing. The art of writing was *one* of the many arts necessary for a manuscript to come into being. The skinner and the parchment maker, the beekeeper who produced the wax tablet, and the painter for the miniatures, were all as necessary as the bookbinder and the lector, or reader, in the copying room. This changed with the division of lines into words. When the copyist saw words in front of him, he was able to copy the original himself, word for word. There is some evidence that in the thirteenth century people who could not read were used for copying because they could copy more accurately.

In Antiquity, even after the great grammarians such as Varro and Quintillian had mastered the word intellectually and were able to teach its forms and functions in the sentence, writing was still pure *grammatika*: a continuous series of letters. Words were strung together without any physical definition. Not until the sequence of letters was read aloud was it possible to grasp the words of the text. The author might in theory dictate a sequence of words; but for the scribe they became an unbroken series of letters. From that series of letters the ear had to extract not only the words but also the elevated rhythm of polished speech.

A very timid beginning at dividing up words was made by Jerome. He interrupted his sequence of letters with *cola* and *commata* in order to make legible some of his translations from the Hebrew that would otherwise have been almost meaningless in Latin. The first strict division of sentences into separate words occurs in the titles of an early manuscript of the *Etymologiae* of Isadore. Division into words first came into common use in the seventh century. It happened at the northern frontiers of the known world, where Celtic "ignoramuses" had to prepare for the priesthood and needed to be taught Latin. Division into words was thus introduced as a means of teaching Latin to barbarians as a foreign language. Like the new pronunciation of Latin, it came to the Continent by way of Tours through Alcuin in the late eighth century. Unlike the new pronunciation, however, which was quickly rejected, the innovation of the word as a visual unit in writing won general acceptance. The ninth century provides us with the first reports of schools beginning to observe *distinctiones*, the spaces between words.

The new graphics of the separated word had an immediate effect on the copying room. Until the eighth century, the writing room was depicted by artists as a dictating room. Then, from the early eighth century, we have a picture of a writing room for which there are no precedents. The scribe sits in front of long strips from which he is copying, although the most usual method of copying was still that of the copier dictating to himself. As early as the ninth century, artists occasionally represented the inspiration of an author—even that of the Evangelists—by showing an angel holding a tome before the writer at his desk; nonetheless, it was not until the thirteenth century that the really radical change occurred.

The writer depicted in early thirteenth-century miniatures no longer holds a knife in his left hand. Instead of writing on the hard leather membrane that had to be smoothed by scraping and sometimes even nailed to the desk with the point of a knife, he now writes on thin parchment and is even beginning to write on paper. His posture is much more relaxed. Writing is no longer strenuous work. His right hand, too, now has an easier job. The writing surface is smooth, the *ductus* flows, and at last the Middle Ages has produced its own cursive script—something that had been forgotten since late Antiquity. The master can now become a writer himself. He is shown with a quill in his hand and not, as he had been for centuries, as a dictator.

Thomas Aquinas, in the middle of the thirteenth century, already had newer writing materials—parchment, penknife, reed, and ink—at his disposal. Drafts in his own hand have come down to us, in the new Gothic cursive which, in its first generation of use, was insufficiently standardized: The master did not yet think that a secretary could copy from his notes. Copying from the master's handwriting by pupils became possible only in the next generation. Thomas still had to dictate in class from his arranged notes, creating his lectures from his written sources. He did not need to limit his notes to a small number of wax tablets. Thomas used notes to assist his trained memory: he drew up a schema of the arguments he was going to deal with. And in many instances, he first dictated his schema and then the execution of it. Earlier teachers did not speak from notes, and they could not check most of their sources.

When Bernard referred to a source he did so from memory. Albertus Magnus and Thomas, two generations later, were the first to have reference books at hand. They quoted verbatim, and after their death, their own works lay chained to library desks, having become reference books in their turn. The new technique of "reference" enables the thirteenth-century author to check his quotations from sources. He can dictate while looking up a passage. The dictator began to have random access to a memory that was laid out before him. Chaucer obviously had before him the text of Boccaccio's *Il Teseide*, as his source, his *auctoritas*, for "The Knight's Tale." The mnemonic devices the rhetorician taught the pupil to build up in his own imagination had taken shape, hundreds of years later, on the page. The Lindisfarne Gospel comes with sixteen pages of canon tables constructed under decorated arches. In the Book of Kells, the fourth-century Eusabian Tables stand at the beginning and suggest to the reader that Matthew, Luke, Mark, and John can be read as one story, since they provide an inkling of the parallels between the four tales. But only in the late twelfth century is this memory device externalized. Any reader can return to any book he has read whenever he wants to do so. And soon it was no longer the works of one's own monastery that the students could reach: the first Union Catalogue came into being shortly after the foundation of the Sorbonne.

Much more significant than the creation of accessible library shelves, however, was the new way of arranging written matter within the book. The art of going back to the exact location of a source of Divine Revelation was from the beginning a necessity that distinguished the Christian from the pagan author. This makes it surprising that the techniques to do so took hundreds of years to be shaped. For a thousand years Holy Scripture was not referred to indirectly, but always *quoted* directly. Saint Augustine had experimented with a device meant to help the readers of the *City of God* find their way about his vast treatise. For this purpose he prepared a *brevicus* as a summary to each of the books. Cassiodorus had experimented in the sixth century with the use of key words as glosses: He extracted them from the text and placed them into the margins as he dictated. Isidore of Seville, just before the Arabs established themselves in southern Spain, first provided his vast *Etymologiae* with chapter headings. But only very slowly did the division of the Bible into chapters become standardized; the division into verses came even more slowly. Gradually the New Testament began to be cited by chapter and verse. Such citation—without the need of quotation—became possible for the Old Testament only after 1200. And then, quite suddenly at the end of the twelfth century, the devices to use the book as a reference tool were there: a subject index to the whole of Holy Scripture. Thus, some 250 years before printing made it possible to refer to the text by page number, a network of grids was laid over the book—a method that had nothing at all to do with the content itself.

During the twelfth century, written texts were visibly fixed in spatial relations to each other. With this text certain elements were made to stand out: Quotations were now written in a different color. The reader's eye, accustomed by the gloss to move from the body to the margin, had to be trained to move from the index to the page, and from one book to the other. Now the eye encompassed not simply the lines, but the entire text. Quite possibly, some of these techniques were developed under Arabic influence. The Moslems, who were not allowed to draw naturalistic pictures, sought to address the eye through the arrangement of letters alone. As a result, Arabic scribes developed a greater variety of colors and diversity of letter arrangements than contemporary Latin books. Certainly the influx of translations from the Arabic—often prepared by Jews from Toledo and Montpellier—inspired some of the new techniques used by the thirteenth-century monks. But Western bookmaking did not become iconoclastic. Precisely as the new methods allowed the text to take visible shape, this text entered into a new relationship to the painted margin and miniatures. Text and illumination are no longer interwoven in the ambiguous manner of Lindisfarne: the patterns do no more than intrude into the lines of the letters, as in the Book of Kells. To describe and to paint have come to be separate tasks often executed by different hands. And yet, the union of illustration and writing during the thirteenth and fourteenth centuries gave rise to the great synthesis of the Western manuscript.

The world now lay described before the reader's eye. The book is now arbitrarily accessible; the reader can enter at will, wherever the index refers him. He sees what is written, and the illustration assists him in this task of visualization. His authorities are perceived as writers rather than as teachers: The "ipse dixit" is replaced by the "ipse scripsit." The pupils now sit in front of their teacher with their eyes fixed on his text, which lies on their knees. They are no more asked to recall the sound of their teacher's words, but to grasp the architecture of his argument, which they must impress on their minds. By the end of the thirteenth century, students in Paris can borrow manuscripts from lending libraries to read with their teachers in class. Libraries become places of silence.

Now truly the reader can say what Hugh of St. Victor had said in 1128: "*Trimodium est lectionis genus: docentis, discentis vel per se inspicientis*" (I can read [aloud] to you, you can read [aloud] to me, and I can read contemplatively to myself). Now reading as an activity of the teacher—in other words, reading aloud—and reading as a listening activity are complemented by a third, silent type of reading: contemplative study of the book.

IV. Translation and Language

In wordless speech there is no word-for-word reproduction of meaning. Writing had fixed neither the language frontier nor the monolingual dependence on translation.

One often forgets that the translator is a frontiersman in more than one sense: He creates the very frontier over which he brings his booty. He is like a ferryman whose boat turns the wild beyond of the barbarous babble into the "other" bank. The translator does not exist in orality. In that world there is neither the dragoman, who hangs about the offices of the Turkish Khadi, nor the Dolmetscher, who sees to it that two texts correspond, nor the "simultaneous parrot" at the United Nations. All these are artisans of the text. They start from the assumption that a person who speaks is, by implication, dictating. It is immaterial whether that dictation is then written down or not because the product of it is in any case a "text." Translation today means turning one text into another. The notion that lies behind it is that texts have a content that is capable of being poured from one vessel—with its own lexical, grammatical, phonetic, and contextual peculiarities—into another.

NE OBSTACLE most modern readers face when they want to study the history of "language" is their belief in monolingual man. From Saussure to Chomsky, "homo monolinguis" is posited as the man who uses language—the man who speaks. This idea had no place in early Greece, or in the Middle Ages; even today it is alien to many people. In their daily life in Java or in the Sahel, a great number of people still feel at home in several kinds of discourse, each of which, to the modern perception, is conducted in a distinct language. But those other people—the Javanese—perceive things differently. They still say "I cannot understand you," rather than "I do not know your language." They are concerned with grasping what the other person has to say by explanation, gesture, or summary; they do not want a translation of that person's statements. As in early Greece, the borders between these cultures, which we moderns are taught to see as "languages," have remained fluid. The idea of "translation" has not yet erected those frontiers that the translator, and only the translator, may bridge.

The eleventh-century cleric who takes down the witness's testimony in the language of the court—who, for example, writes in Latin what the witness says in Swabian—is a scribe. He has no intention to translate. Neither is the bishop translating who reads out the homily in accordance with the rules of the Council of Tours: He teaches by announcing the word of God and interpreting it. He is helping people understand. But that is a long way from translating.

Even today, we often say: "Help me, would you—I'd like to understand what the old man or the scientist is saying." Surely, we are not seeking a translator, but someone to help us understand—an interpreter. We rely on the intermediary who understands the mutterings of an old woman, the dialect of Lower Bavaria, scientific language, or Chinese. The question "What did he say?" contains the request "Tell me what he is trying to tell me." We do not even expect our companion to have understood word for word; we only want to under-

53

stand what *he* has understood. This understanding of explanations, coupled with the ability to explain what one has understood, is basic to oral discourse.

For the idealistic language inmate of a language prison this type of intercourse has become either inconceivable or irritating. He finds it hard to accept that the phenomenon to which he refers by the term "language" has a history—that it was once socially created and may also pass away. Just as the word assumed its present form through writing, so did "language" assume its present form through the translation of texts.

According to George Steiner, translation did not become an issue in the period before Christ. The few literate people were usually bilingual, and for the others, what was said in one language could be retold, summed up, reported, or commented on in the other. Cicero and Horace were among the first to refer to translation as an art. The Greek work was not to be turned into Latin *verbum pro verbo*. Instead, the meaning was to be detached from the words of one language and made to reappear in another; content, stripped of its form, was to be preserved. Theories about translation changed very little—translation was described as an attempt to divulge the secrets of one language into another—until the hermeneutics of the 1950s. Only then did the study of translation as applied linguistic theory become separated from literary theory. In the end, we would agree with Borges: "Ninguna problema tan consustancial con los letras y con su modesto misterio como el que propone una traduccion" (Translation reflects what is most uncanny about literacy).

The absence of theory did not hamper the Middle Ages from growing into an age of translation. The age of translation begins, not only with the Christian desire to preach the Gospel to all people, but to appropriate its Hebrew and Greek books into the culture of late Antiquity, which, in the West with Augustine, became monolingual. Saint Jerome defined his activity as translator in an image to which the monks of Reichenau made allusion: "Quasi captivos sensus in suam linguam victoris iure transposuit" ("As the victor deports his prisoners under the rule of war, so [the translator] carries meaning over into his own language"). And precisely because Jerome was aware of the violence done to the text by translation, he called for limits to be set to the process. He preferred to tolerate meaningless sequences of words in his Latin Bible than have what he regarded as something inexpressible obscured by interpretation: "Alioquin et multa alia quae ineffabilia sunt, et humanus animus capere non potest, hac licentia delebuntur."

Translation in the Middle Ages carried a unique significance because of the unique status of Latin—the only language used in writing. Latin became the only vessel out of which divine revelation could be drawn. By the time of Charlemagne, it had joined Greek and Hebrew as a holy language out of which translation could be made.

Monks in the ninth century began to fashion *theotisc* into a vessel into which they would dare to pour the content of Latin scripture. To enable translations to be made from the now holy Latin language, in Murbach and on the island of Reichenau, the shaping of the German language became an object of scholarly attention. Within less than a generation, these monks had fashioned a German vocabulary that bore comparison with that of Latin, in order to translate their Benedictine Rule. Glossaries were composed in order to find verbal counterparts for "the last filtration of Latin thought and literary discipline." Through considered new coinings, through precise definition of new fields of meaning, through loan syntax or paronymous new coinings, something entirely new came into being: From German tongues there crystallized a German language that could be regarded as an equivalent of Latin.

From the middle of the ninth century, a single document written in the Romance language has come down to us, and it happens to be an oath. This Romance text is included in a chronicle written by Nithard in what for the period is unusually good Latin. Nithard, who succeeded his father as Abbot of St. Riquier, was a grandson of Charlemagne through his mother Berta. He served another grandson of Charlemagne, Charles the Bald. He wrote his chronicle at the age of nineteen—two years before his death in battle in 844. In lively terms he describes things that he himself experienced. He complains about the decline of the Holy Roman Empire and that particular year's poor weather. We know from his chronicle that in 841 Charles the Bald and Louis the German conspired against their brother Lothar. Nithard wrote down the oaths of both the rulers and their men by which this conspiracy was effected. Each ruler took an oath on behalf of himself and his men in the other's language.

Both vernacular oaths were based on an ingenious Latin original that may possibly have been drawn up by Nithard for his master and cousin, but that has not survived. These two versions, known as the Strasbourg Oaths, played crucial though very different roles in the history of the French and German languages.

The text in *romana lingua* is the earliest alphabetic representation of colloquial speech in France. For something like a thousand years a dialect had been spoken in France that lent itself perfectly to notation in Latin characters but was never written.

The "vulgar" living speech of tradesmen, craftsmen, women, and public officials that survived in France for thirty generations is unknown to us. Like Latin, it had come from Italy, but it took root earlier and remained far longer than Latin. However, as in Lombardy and on the Iberian Peninsula, it was neither distinguished from Latin as a separate "language," nor was it ever written down.

Precise analysis of the Romance text of the Strasbourg Oaths shows beyond any doubt that Nithard's text is not a transcription of a spoken language. It constitutes an attempt to take a carefully worked-out formula, written and conceived in Latin, and to adapt it phonetically and syntactically to the Alsatian mode of expression. The text is a remarkable example of an already developed juridical terminology in learned and complex syntax, with a stilted technical vocabulary, that corresponds exactly to the Latin oaths of Carolingian princes that have come down to us. The conspiracy of the Carolingian princes here became an opportunity to have an army solemnly repeat a text that had been read aloud to them in a facsimile of their own dialect.

The dialect was not a "Latin" dialect. Even by the time of the eruption of Vesuvius in 79 A.D., the Romans were no longer speaking the way Latin was spelled. The volcanic ash preserved graffiti that people had daubed on the walls of their houses. The word structure of these uneducated scrawls shows signs of shifts that, up until recently, philologists assumed took place a thousand years later. In words ending with *m*, for instance, the final *m* is often dropped. Probably the *m* was either not pronounced at all or was fused with the preceding vowel to form a nasal—as occurs in present-day Portuguese. Many researchers believe that this gap between language as it was spoken and language as it was spelled was by no means confined to the poorer classes. The Classical poetry of the period takes on a fresh charm when the *m* is swallowed—as in Brazilian. And, in 841—seven hundred years after Vesuvius—the Romance spoken in Gaul, like that spoken in Iberia, had moved much farther away from Latin word structure. What was read approximated the local form of *lingua romana*. For the reader, word structure was determined by grammar, and pronunciation by the landscape. In many places, Latin pronunciation was probably as far removed from orthography as is modern English.

Among the aims of the Carolingian reform had been to have Latin read—and consequently also spoken—in a uniform manner throughout the empire. Charlemagne wished to match the existing unity of spelling with a unity of sound. Such an objective would today tend to be regarded as a call for mutual understanding. But such a change was certainly not necessary for mutual understanding at the time. Every monk learned the Latin pronunciation of his own monastery. If he walked from Subiaco to Fulda, his feet bore him no faster than his ear was able to adjust itself to new pronunciations, just as today's Indian pilgrim still finds his ear adjusting to the landscape with every step he takes. Moreover, despite big differences in accents—today we should say languages—people's readiness to listen and to understand is far greater in a traditional society than present-day schoolteachers imagine. For more than a thousand years, in some sense, Latin lived.

Charlemagne and his circle of educated monks—Peter the Grammarian, from whom the adult emperor would have liked to learn to write; Paulinus, whose hymns are today still sung in the chancel office; Paul the Deacon, the court historian; the Spaniard, West-Goth Theodolf, wit and art expert; the layman Einhard, Charlemagne's biographer—all of these men together had no less an aim than to mold all the peoples of the empire into a univocal congregation. Sovereignty was interpreted as a gift from God in the service of the Church. Visible unification and standardization of all spheres of life had a symbolic rather than a practical purpose: to correct ingrained habits according to the original text. Mythical "ur-texts" were sought for the Latin Bible, for canon law, for the liturgy, and for monastic life. The plan to standardize Latin pronunciation needs to be seen in the same context, that is to say, as a theologically motivated attempt to create a symbolically effective, uniform, imperial, dead "language"—not to improve a "means of communication."

On the Continent, no one would have carried out such a plan. The idea that a uniform written language demanded a uniform pronunciation contradicted a basic belief of the Church. The Book of Revelation was one, and had to be understood by all people, each in his own tongue; in the daily performance of this feat, the miracle of Pentecost was constantly repeated. This "miracle" could be performed everywhere in England except in those areas where Romance had never been used as the vernacular, which made it possible for the "correct" pronunciation of written Latin to become a research subject in the eighth century. The Venerable Bede wrote a treatise on orthography. Alcuin the Scot—born in the year of Bede's death (736) and raised among his pupils—

was summoned to Charlemagne's court as schoolmaster and placed in charge of the school in Tours. He came from a tradition in which Classical education was rooted, not in the continuity of the *lingua romana*, but in the continuity that stemmed from the systematic adoption of Latin in the monastery and in the liturgy.

Charlemagne relied on Alcuin to unify the pronunciation of Latin. Unlike his Continental brothers, when Alcuin read a text, he pronounced it as a dead language. He trained his pupils to read Latin the way he had learned to read it in York, with each letter being given its correct value—that is to say, pronounced with the same sound each time. This concern for uniform pronunciation was even reflected in the contractions that appeared in the new, standard Carolingian handwriting. Repeatedly, only that part of a word is written that the Franks would otherwise have stressed insufficiently or swallowed altogether. Forty years before the Strasbourg Oaths, then, Alcuin's school was deliberately trying to make the "reading" of Latin incomprehensible to the vernacular ear. Only in this context can one understand how it could have occurred to Nithard to write *lingua romana* phonetically.

Alcuin's phonetic reform was meant to breathe new life into Latin. The immediate consequence, however, was that Latin became incomprehensible to the listener when read aloud. The Carolingian *renovatio* constituted an obstacle to the Church's preaching. A year before Charlemagne's death the Church's rejection of his unhistorical concept of correct pronunciation found expression at the Council of Tours— the very town in which Alcuin had taught only a few years before. It forbade priests to use the new way of reading during services. The Council enjoins the celebrant to read from this book written in Latin, but to strive in the process to speak in the Romance or *theotisc* vernacular. Priests in the province of Tours were to continue doing what they had always done without criticism. On the basis of the Latin texts, they were to read out what their congregations could understand.

The argument between advocates of a revived Latin and the Church's priests hinged on the interpretation of what kind of activity "reading" should be—should it be the spelling out of the letters that correspond to the sounds of a long-dead language, or should it be the transformation of the lines into their own living speech? With this canon, the Council of Tours was reacting against putting a lower limit on standard literary language. Alcuin's idea of Latin implied one formal set of phonetics for the entire Empire. That new phonetics posed a threat to the function of Latin writing, which was to serve all peoples (*gentes*).

"Easdem omelias quisque aperte transferre studeat in rusticam romanam linguam aut theotiscam, quo facilius possint intellegere quae dicuntur," proclaimed the bishops assembled at Tours. The council wished to hold the door open for congregations to understand the text (*quo facilius possint intellegere*). It therefore required the reader to take pains (*studeat*) to pronounce what he was reading (*quae dicuntur*) in such a way that the collection of Latin texts (*omeliae*) intended to help elucidate the scriptures came across in a manner people could understand (*aperte transferre . . . in rusticam linguam*), no matter if that "language" in which the Latin text is read out of is German or French. The emphasis here is on the *rusticam*: The reader was to do his reading in a vernacular, rustic manner.

A B C

Two such tongues (*linguae*) are mentioned: *romana* and *theo-tisca*. Thus, by changing pronunciation (tongue), one could change the Latin, read aloud, into German or French.

Contemporary usage suggests an opposition between German and French because we think in terms of "languages" as self-contained systems of communication that may be compared one with another, but only in the context of their separateness. Neither this modern notion of a neatly defined language, nor that of equivalent language can be projected into a ninth-century text. The *aut* between *romana* and *theotisca* has much more to do with a polarity than with an either/or sense of exclusion. In the same way as the Council opposed the cultivation of a contradiction between the reading aloud of Latin and a generally comprehensible manner of speaking, this canon is talking, not about a translation process, but about a reading process. Reading aloud comprehensibly—however the book is written—is something different from translating Latin into Old French or Old High German.

This can be elucidated by considering the word *theotisc*. It was not until shortly before 800 that this word started to become remolded from "popular" to "of German origin," and *theotisca lingua* from "people's speech" to "Germanic." The efforts of the monks at Reichenau, Fulda, and in Alsace to create the rudiments of a German language gave rise to the idea that *theotisc* was a language distinct from Latin, potentially equivalent to but heterogenous from it, out of and into which it was possible to translate. However, this idea had not yet won general acceptance. And vernacular languages were still far from being the separate and distinct cages in which we today think we are locked.

Up until the time of the earliest vernacular grammars—

in other words, up until the late fifteenth century—*lingua* or *tongue* or *habla* was less like one drawer in a bureau than one color in a spectrum. The comprehensibility of speech was comparable to the intensity of a color. Just as one color may appear with greater or lesser intensity, may bleed into its neighbor, just as landscapes merge into one another, so it is with the Council's *aut* in relation to *romanam* and *theotiscam*. Latin stands in contrast to both "tongues" because it is an orthographic "language." But so long as there was no compulsion to read aloud in an orthophonetic manner, the reader was free to paint the meaning of what he was reading in any color of the rainbow. And it was on this Christian tradition of a logogrammatical reading of a text written in phonetic notation that the canons of Tours insisted.

By determining the nature of reading in this way, Christianity dissociated itself from the temple at an early stage. As reported by a first-century Jewish source—the Megillah Teanith (The Fasting Scroll)—three days of darkness came over the earth on the day the seventy wise Jews completed their Greek translation of the Torah, the Septuagint. Even today the Koran may not be translated from the Arabic. Christian preaching consists precisely of the fact that every foreigner in Jerusalem was able to hear the Hebrew message in his own native language. Public, vocal meditation during reading is of the essence to the Christian message. The modulation on each syllable that characterizes Gregorian plainchant and the vernacular annunciation of the Gospel are the two extreme forms. Without an appreciation for Mnemosyne it is impossible either to understand the Christian concepts of devout reading, or to grasp what it means that God became the Word that unfolds in Scripture. In the context of these multiple forms of reading, the doctrine of the four-fold interpretation of the sacred text reached its height.

According to the evidence of the Strasbourg Oaths, however, ideogrammatical reading since the ninth century effected precisely the opposite result. The text that Nithard has preserved does not render what anyone had actually said. The work of a wily chaplain, this cunningly devised chunk of speech became the language in which the chancellory took possession of ancient forms of oath. Alliteration and strong words make the army pay due heed to an unaccustomed vow. Every fighting man was to repeat those sentences after a verbatim recital by a cleric. The sentence structure and phraseology of the Romance version show clearly that this intrusion of stilted Latin formulae into the Romance vernacular was not new in Nithard's day; some set forms of its wording give the impression of having been already polished by chancery use. The oaths provide an example of the manner in which letters can shape people, not only before anyone can trace or decipher them, but before a single song or statement has been written in that people's vernacular. The oath is just one of several ways in which the unwritten literature of popular culture was learned by heart. The memorization of prayers was probably much more effective. Even in the thirteenth century, confession still served as a means for the clergy to see if individuals knew the Pater and the Creed by heart.

The medieval clergy's habit of taking depositions in the vernacular and writing them down in Latin, and reading Latin oaths, creeds, and statements by formulating them in vernacular utterances that the people had to repeat, throws light on why epic poetry so rarely came to be written down as it was sung. Unlike the Greek scribe who wrote down what he heard "Homer" sing, the Roman cleric wrote down in Latin what he had understood. And when, on occasion, he wrote it down in the vernacular, the literate scribe was trained to "improve" the version as he wrote it down.

Another landmark in the history of language occurred on August 18, 1492—just fifteen days after Columbus had set sail—when a Spaniard named Elio Antonio de Nebrija published the first grammar in any modern European language, the *Gramática Castellana*, which attempted to reduce a vernacular tongue to rules of grammar. Nebrija goes beyond the Carolingian scribe, who listened to Frankish depositions and wrote them down in Latin. He demands that Spanish be made into a language that is not spoken, but that serves to record speech.

The six-page introduction to the *Gramática* presents a concise and powerful argument why the new age, dawning when Columbus departed, called for the replacement of the vernacular speech of the people by a language—an "artifact"—that all people must henceforth be taught. At this time the Spanish monarchs were engaged in transforming the idea of government. They replaced the old aristocratic advisory bodies by organizations of well-lettered officials. Just recently, and only for a few years, the Crown had seized the Inquisition from the Church, thereby acquiring the power needed to dislodge the sword-carrying nobility who were to be replaced by men of the pen. The conception of government as the machinery that guarantees the execution of the monarch's utterance was now reshaped into one that prepares texts for his signature. The state governed by the management of texts—

that is, the modern bureaucratic state—was taking shape. And, under the Hapsburgs, in the late sixteenth century, the transformation became ritually visible. "Ministeriales," high-level scribes, were assigned ritual roles in the court cere-monial of processions and liturgies, often outranking the men of the sword. Nebrija addresses this new secular balance be-tween *armas y letras*. He argues with the queen for a new pact between sword and book and proposes a covenant between two spheres—both within the secular realm of the Crown—a covenant distinct from the medieval pact between Emperor and Pope, which had been a covenant bridging the secular and the sacred.

Very astutely, Nebrija reminds the queen that a new union of *armas y letras*, complementary to that of Church and State, was essential for gathering and joining the scattered pieces of Spain into a single absolute kingdom:

This unified and sovereign body will be of such shape and inner cohesion that centuries will be unable to undo it. Now that the Church has been purified, and we are thus reconciled to God, now that the enemies of the Faith have been subdued by our arms, now that just laws are being enforced, enabling us all to live as equals, what else remains but the flowering of the peaceful arts. And among the arts, foremost are those of language, which sets us apart from the wild animals; language, which is the unique distinction of man, the means for the kind of understanding which can be surpassed only by contemplation.

Continuing to develop his petition, Nebrija introduces the crucial element of his argument: *La lengua suelta y fuera de regla*—the unbound and ungoverned speech in which people actually live and manage their lives has become a challenge to the Crown. Nebrija thus interprets an unproblematic historical fact as a problem for the architects of a new kind of polity—the modern state:

Your majesty, it has been my constant desire to see our nation become great, and to provide the men of my tongue with books worthy of their leisure. Presently, they waste their time on novels and fancy stories full of lies.

An argument for standardized language is also made today, but the end is now different. Our contemporaries believe that standardized language is a necessary condition to teach people to read, indispensable for the distribution of printed books. Nebrija argues just the opposite: He was upset because people who spoke in dozens of distinct vernacular tongues in 1492 had become the victims of a reading epidemic. They wasted their leisure on books that circulated outside of any possible bureaucratic control. Manuscripts had been so rare and precious that authorities could often suppress the work of an author by literally seizing *all* the copies, burning them and extirpating the text. Not so books. Even with the small edition of two hundred to a thousand copies—typical for the first generation of print—it was never possible to confiscate an entire run. Printed books called for the exercise of censorship through an *Index of Forbidden Books*. Books could only be proscribed, not destroyed. But Nebrija's proposal appeared more than fifty years before the first *Index* was published in 1599. And he wished to achieve control over the printed word on a much deeper level than that later attempted by the Church. He wanted to replace the people's vernacular with the grammarian's language. The humanist proposes the standardization of colloquial language to re-move the new technology of printing from the vernacular do-main—to prevent people from printing and reading in the various languages that, up to that time, they had only spoken. By this monopoly over an official and taught language, he pro-poses to suppress wild, untaught vernacular reading.

To grasp the full significance of Nebrija's argument—that compulsory education in a standardized national mother tongue is necessary to prevent people from wanton, plea-sureful reading—one must remember the status of print at that time. Nebrija was born before the appearance of move-able type. He was thirteen when the first moveable stock came into use. His conscious adult life coincides with the incunab-ula. When printing was in its twenty-fifth year, he published his Latin grammar; in its thirty-fifth, he published his Spanish grammar. Nebrija could recall the time before print—as many of us can recall the time before television. Nebrija's text was by coincidence published the year William Caxton died.

The last paragraph of Nebrija's introduction exudes elo-quence. Evidently, the teacher of rhetoric knew what he taught. Nebrija has explained his project; given the queen logical reasons to accept it; frightened her with what would happen if she were not to heed him. Finally, like Columbus, he appeals to her sense of a manifest destiny:

Now, Your Majesty, let me come to the last advantage that you shall gain from my grammar. For the purpose, recall the time when I presented you with a draft of this book earlier this year in Sala-manca. At this time, you asked me what end such a grammar could possibly serve. Upon this, the Bishop of Avila interrupted to an-swer in my stead. What he said was this: "Soon Your Majesty will have placed her yoke upon many barbarians who speak outlandish tongues. By this, your victory, these people shall stand in a new need; the need for the laws the victor owes to the vanquished, and the need for the language we shall bring with us." My grammar shall serve to impart them the Castilian tongue, as we have used grammar to teach Latin to our young.

We can attempt a reconstruction of what happened at Salamanca when Nebrija handed the queen a draft of his forthcoming book. The queen praised the humanist for having provided the Castilian tongue with what had been reserved to the languages of Scripture, Hebrew, Greek, and Latin. But while Isabella was able to grasp the achievement of her *letrado*—the description of a living tongue as rules of grammar—she was unable to see any practical use for such an undertaking. For her, grammar was an instrument designed solely for use by teachers. She believed, moreover, that the vernacular simply could not be taught. In her royal view of linguistics, every subject of her many kingdoms was so made by nature that during his lifetime he would reach perfect dominion over his own tongue *on his own*. In this version of "majestic linguistics," the vernacular is the *subject's* domain. By the very nature of things, the vernacular is beyond the reach of the ruler's authority.

Isabella's initial rejection of Nebrija's proposal underscores its originality. Nebrija argued against a traditional and typically Iberian prejudice of Isabella—the notion that the Crown cannot encroach on the variety of customs in the kingdoms—and called up the image of a new, universal mission for a *modern* Crown. Nebrija overcame Isabella's prejudices by promising to serve her mystical mission. First, he argued that the vernacular must be replaced by an *artificio* to give the monarch's power increased range and duration; then, to cultivate the arts by decision of the court; also to guard the established order against the threat presented by wanton reading and printing. But he concluded his petition with an appeal to the "Grace of Granada," the queen's destiny, not just to conquer, but to civilize the entire world.

Both Columbus and Nebrija offered their services to a new kind of empire builder. But Columbus proposed only to use the recently created caravels to the limit of their range for the expansion of royal power in what would become New Spain. Nebrija's appeal was more basic—he argued the use of his grammar for the expansion of the Queen's power in a totally new sphere that he proposed to create through the act of conquest itself. He intended the creation of the sphere of a taught mother tongue—the first invented part of universal education.

Columbus was to open the way to the New World; Nebrija devised a way to control Spanish subjects by providing a way to standardize their language.

v. The Self

*The practical concern in the thirteenth century with the identity of
two charters and the spiritual concern with the individuality of each
person reflect the new ability to distinguish what is in the book and
what is on the page. The word* individual *itself comes from Antiquity. In Porphyry's* Commentaries on Aristotelian categories, *the
word carries the meaning of "unambiguousness"; it has a deictic
or demonstrative character. It means an ultimately indivisible (a-
tomos) something, the subject of which something is predicated—
for example, Socrates, to whom we can point as the "bearded, gar-
rulous, son of so-and-so." In this sense,* in-dividuum *(Cicero's
translation of* a-tomos*) was carried over the bridge of Isidore of
Seville's* Etymologiae *into the Middle Ages. Abelard used the word
in the same deictic sense. Albert the Great took the "individual"
beyond Classical Antiquity when he grasped the difference between
the* individuum vaguum *and the* individuum certum, *the frog
whose croaking woke him up last night, as opposed to this particular
croaker that I catch and am able to skewer.*

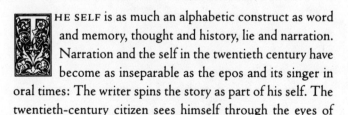HE SELF is as much an alphabetic construct as word
and memory, thought and history, lie and narration.
Narration and the self in the twentieth century have
become as inseparable as the epos and its singer in
oral times: The writer spins the story as part of his self. The
twentieth-century citizen sees himself through the eyes of

various sciences as a layer cake of texts. From the eighteenth century on, the state has become a corporation of selves that letters examine.

No language can get by without a first person singular, which in some languages is demonstrative—for example, the Hebrew *ani* that acts like a finger turned backwards—and in other languages sets the speaker off from the rest. But, unlike the "I," most epochs got along without a self. There was no self in epic times. According to Bruno Snell, there was not even a body: heroes refer to their arm or their "thymos," but do not contextualize these into the kind of body we now have. In oral cultures, one may retain an image of what has been— yesterday, at the time of the full moon, or last spring, but the person then or now exists only in the doing or the telling, as the suffix comes to life only when it modifies a verb. Like a candle, the "I" lights up only in the activity and is extinguished at other times. But not dead. With the retelling of the story, the candle comes to glow again. No pilot light gives continuity to the first person singular between one story and the next. The "I" can exist only in the act of speaking out loud—or to oneself.

The idea of a self that continues to glimmer in thought or memory, occasionally retrieved and examined in the light of day, cannot exist without the text. Where there is no alphabet, there can neither be a memory conceived as a storehouse nor the "I" as its appointed watchman. With the alphabet both text and self became possible, but only slowly, and they became the social construct on which we found all our perceptions as literate people.

Writing the history of the self is as difficult as writing the history of the text. The self is a cloth we have been weaving over centuries in confessions, journals, diaries, memories, and in its most literate incarnation, the autobiography, to tailor the dress in which we see our first person singular. *Beowulf* dates from the life of Bede (671–735), the time that the Christian alphabet came to England; its hero, Beowulf, has nothing of what we moderns call "self." But by the fourteenth century it is clear that to the two books delineated by someone like St. Bonaventure—the Book of Creation and the Scriptures—has been added a third: the Book of the Self. Hugh of St. Cher refers to the Book of the Heart, which, at the end of time, Hugh declares, Christ will open to reveal all "things secret." Alanus de Insulis calls man's conscience a book hiding things of the soul. These secrets too will be revealed on the Day of Judgement. And in the next several centuries, the self becomes an established literary phenomenon that can be read in popular accounts such as Benvenuto Cellini's supposed autobiography, Rousseau's *Confessions*, and the interminable memoirs of Casanova. At virtually the same moment that James Boswell is lionizing his friend Samuel Johnson, through the biography, Benjamin Franklin is doing the same thing for himself, in his autobiography—though he uses the old term, *memoir*. It is also in America that the newly constituted self quietly reaches its crisis, with Henry Adams.

We cannot conceive facing each other except as selves. The image of the self that we have inherited seems to us fundamental for western culture. But we notice that some of our students are bred on electronic text composers. "Text" means something entirely different for them than it does for us. And thus we sense its extreme fragility at this moment. We fear that the image of the self made in the image of the text could fade from society, together with the self-destruction of the text. Retracing the sociogenesis of our perception, we want to point to its historical nature.

In three thousand lines, *Beowulf* describes the wondrous adventures of Beowulf, whose patronymic translates as Bee-Wolf, or simply Bear. Like a bear, Beowulf swims vigorously, runs swiftly, and fights fiercely. He possesses the strength of thirty men in his right hand. A mighty animal is his model; though he is quasi-human, the hero is not inarticulate. Indeed, he is adept at reconstructing his genealogical roots: he does so in over fifty lines of well-shaped verse. With deftness he tells the story of his prodigious three-day swimming contest with Breca. The same story about the contest with Breca is told by Unferth completely differently. What to us looks like a contradiction in the two stories never becomes a "problem" for Beowulf and is never "resolved." Unferth's diverging story merely shows Beowulf in another light. Beowulf knows no hesitation, he cannot lie, but neither can he take inventory of his life. He seems incapable of remembering. He suffers no pangs of conscience, no regrets. Larger than life, he is also far removed from it.

However, during the last hours of *Beowulf*, on the third and final day of his struggle with the dragon, a kink occurs in the story; for eight and one-half lines there is talk of a kind of shame or guilt or causality—what we would not know how to call anything but "conscience." Less than one hundred lines from the end of the poem a young warrior, named Wiglaf, the sole survivor of an ancient tribe called the Waegmundings, sounds this new and discordant note. He chides his comrades for not aiding their king, who has kept them secure for so many years, in his own time of need in this fatal fight with the dragon.

The death of Beowulf signals more than the simple end of a ruler; it marks the passing away of the heroic way of life and the spirit of *comitatus* (community) that holds that life together. Young Wiglaf represents the new order in the poem. Perhaps Wiglaf is a Christian interpolation by some monastic scribe, but nonetheless his voice is a new one in English. He wants those cowardly old men to feel bad, and he wants them to carry that feeling around with them. So he scolds:

> Wergendra tō lȳt
> þrong ymbe þēoden, þā hyne sīo þrāg becwōm.
> Nū sceal sinc-þego ond swyrd-gifu,
> eall ēð el-wyn ēowrum cynne,
> lufen ālicgean; lond-rihtes mōt
> þǣre mæg-burge monna ǣghwylc
> īdel hweorfan, syððan æðelingas
> feorran gefricgean flēam ēowerne,
> dōm-lēasan dǣd. Dēað bið sēlla
> eorla gehwylcum þonne edwīt-līf.

> (Too few defenders
> pressed round the king when his worst time came.
> Now all treasure, giving and receiving,
> all home-joys, ownership, comfort,
> shall cease for your kin; deprived of their rights
> each man of your families will have to be exiled,
> once nobles afar hear of your flight,
> a deed of no glory. Death is better
> for any warrior than a shameful life!)

Embarrassed and ashamed—and still too frightened to fight—they do the only thing left to them: skulk off to the woods.

But Wiglaf will not allow the Waegmundings to forget their betrayal. He wants those warriors to be stuck with their guilt or their shame—or both. Wiglaf implies that each of those men possesses something like a self whose voice is his conscience. He sends a messenger to court to foretell the horror of the feuds that will be caused by their cowardly inaction. For the first and only time in the entire poem, past action is presented as the cause of future grief. Wiglaf interprets the history of feuding tribes as the result of the guilt of forebears.

Beowulf is then set on a barge, along with all his treasures. Set afire, the barge drifts off to some unknown destination. Women bewail a past epoch and keen over the king. The future looms in grim detail. Wiglaf has erased the present. Warriors are helpless to undo the past while they prepare for what is to come. For the present they can only lament and hide.

James Cox, a literary critic concerned with autobiography, argues convincingly that autobiography is not only an American invention, but one that flourishes, as nowhere else, in America. Franklin, the Ur-American portrait of success—founder of a university, a hospital, a library, a philosophical society, the postal system; inventor of the stove, the smokeless street lamp, bifocals, electrical conduction, and the glass harmonica, among other things—"at the age of sixty-five embarked upon what one wants to call his great invention—the invention of himself, not as a fiction, but as a fact and in history." Thus, in Franklin we are not reading some fictional character like Lancelot, or some product of romantic longing like Casanova, but a fictional fact.

In the *Confessions*, Augustine realizes that hubris must inevitably end in failure; he must, therefore, eschew the things of this world. But autobiography is born out of hubris, it requires that the self be woven into the very design of material society. In Franklin's case, his autobiography grows out of the hubris of America's emerging power—its myths and ideals—a power that actually thrives on mistakes. One merely seizes upon them, as Franklin makes clear, and turns them into substantial financial success. Autobiography amplifies that power: Since a person is literally creating a new being, he can smooth out the rough transitions in his life, clean up the mistakes, to produce a polished and attractive literary self. The writer presents his life as he thinks it should have been. Thus, every autobiography is in some ways a declaration of independence, as the writer bids farewell to his baggy historical self, embracing a new, tidy, authorized, and public one. It marks an act of willful liberation. No wonder, then, the number of powerful American black autobiographies, such as the *Narrative of Frederick Douglass*, *The Autobiography of Malcolm X*, the story of George Washington Carver, and the *Confessions of Nat Turner*. How fitting that Franklin, so concerned with autobiography, should have been one of the framers of the Declaration of Independence. He was also President of the Executive Council of Pennsylvania, as well as a delegate to the Constitutional Convention. And in his *Autobiography* Franklin continually measures himself against that singularly American founding document, the Constitution.

Constitution is a word that had been in use for only a hundred or a hundred and fifty years by 1771, the year Franklin began writing his memoirs, to mean the composition of some body or some thing; and Franklin borrows the idea to help enact the "constitution of his own self." This self should not be seen as a mere literary fabrication, Franklin implies, but in some substantive way "constituted" out of the homely virtues of honesty, sobriety, moderation, frugality, and perseverance. A self so constituted knows no limits to its accomplishments: Like everyone else, Franklin pursued life, liberty, and happiness and he shows that hard work pays off in enormous success.

Franklin's *Autobiography* charts his climb from raggedy beginnings, in the guise of the frugal and industrious Poor Richard (Saunders), through an encyclopedic and disparate series of selves, to the birth of that star, the Great Doctor Franklin. While the *Autobiography* breaks off its narration in 1757, the moment that Franklin's career really takes off, John Adams points out that when Franklin began writing the *Autobiography* he was already an international celebrity: "There was scarcely a citizen who was not familiar with his name and who did not consider him a friend to human kind."

Poor Richard, it turns out, is rich in wisdom, which he expresses in pithy sayings and maxims. Franklin sprinkles them throughout the *Autobiography*: A penny saved is a tuppence clear; God helps those who help themselves; A word to the wise is enough. Collected and sold in little pamphlets, Richard's advice became a commodity easily dispensed and digested, a constant reminder of the importance of practical application. Those apothegms helped to mask the real-life Franklin, a sometimes untidy, spendthrift man, at loose ends with his own finances. But more than that, Richard Saunders sired Ben Franklin, a *brand*-new self—we still refer to *Franklin* stoves, *Franklin* glasses, *Franklin* lightning rods. (Franklin patented none of his inventions, saying that "as we enjoy great advantage from the inventions of others, we should be glad of an opportunity to serve others by any invention of ours."

Curiously enough, American patent law derives from a provision in the Constitution empowering Congress "to promote the progress of science and useful arts by securing . . . to inventors the exclusive right to their . . . discoveries.") A public self like Franklin's is essential for the full-time pursuit of success. The question may be: How long can the pursuit be sustained?

The answer is delivered in the next century, with *The Education of Henry Adams*, considered by most historians to be the first autobiography, one in which we can actually experience a self crystallizing around the act of writing. We see the struggles and the mistakes; we are present at the moment of crisis. Franklin writes from a position of solid success; he's already made it, and from this position of assuredness glances over his shoulder to document its history. Adams writes out of failure.

The Education of Henry Adams involves a dialogue between the failed Adams, who hopes to learn from his mistakes, and some other Adams. To make this clear, Adams adopts a curious literary stance: *The Education* is the life of Henry Adams told by Henry Adams, but narrated in the third person. We are thus made to experience two Adamses: the previous one—actually Adams as a young man—and the new Adams—the writer as an older man. Not only are there two Adamses, however, but more curiously, the young Adams, the literary creation being remembered, or recollected, takes on its own life and begins to educate the new Adams.

Here is a truly extraordinary development: The literary creation of the self has assumed enough life of its own to instruct and educate its creator. This third-person golem must be disposed of, dealt with, or, ideally, incorporated back into the first person. The young Adams in fact controls the situation so strongly that he turns the old Adams, the writer, into a ghostly fictional character. Adams must figure out how to take back his life. So these two selves travel the entire meandering path of the book as master/pupil; they stand together at the moment of crisis in Paris on April 15, 1900, at the largest exhibition ever held in Europe, the Great Exposition.

Ben Franklin ransacked his soul to uncover there the multifarious parts of his soul—artist, printer, inventor, educator, designer, statesman, scientist, and so on. Some powerful invisible force drove Franklin toward success. At the Great Exposition, Adams saw that force updated and made concrete in one grand contraption: the forty-foot-high dynamos displayed in the Gallery of Machines.

For Adams, the Virgin represented the great religious symbol of the twelfth century; for the twentieth century, that symbol was the dynamo. Both stand as "revelations of a mysterious energy like that of the Cross; they were what in terms of medieval science were called immediate modes of the divine substance," symbols of a continuing divine force that has driven the history of man. Just like the Virgin, the dynamo was capable of attracting untold numbers of followers. Puzzling over the connection between these two disparate centuries, Adams begins to perceive the possibilities of education anew; indeed, a hazardous one: "The knife-edge along which he must crawl, like Sir Lancelot in the twelfth century, divided two kingdoms of force which had nothing in common but attraction."

The new Adams learns from the old Adams that the great invisible force of the twentieth century—producing electricity, X rays, and radium—has been around forever, just like the force of Christianity. At times, this force becomes visible. The Virgin represented a form of faith still felt at Lourdes, at the Louvre, and at Chartres. There, as he knew by the record of work he still could see, existed "the highest energy ever known to man, the creator of four-fifths of his noblest art, exercising vastly more attraction over the human mind than all the steam-engines and dynamos ever dreamed of; and yet this energy was unknown to the American mind. An American virgin would never dare command; an American Venus would never dare exist." Through the dynamo, Adams reckons, the American mind would finally be able to grasp the immensity of a divine force. America tottered on the verge of momentous change, which Adams, in his excitement, can only equate with other revolutionary moments: "Copernicus and Galileo had broken many professional necks about 1600; Columbus had stood the world on its head towards 1500; but the nearest approach to the revolution of 1900 was that of 310, when Constantine set up the Cross."

In yet another reversal in *The Education*, Adams understands as he actually stands under this dynamo the great lesson of his education: he is a failure. Not that Adams was not born of the proper Brahman, New England stock, not that he had failed to attend the correct schools, or that he had not created elegant and influential works of literature, like the wonderfully seductive *Mont-Saint-Michel and Chartres*, but that he had failed in the invisible world of the spirit.

Ironically, Adams had created his self with so much clarity and precision—the young Adams had been too much of a literary success—that his current state of failure becomes painfully clear to him. Adams has interpreted the self, analyzed it, and what he finds the literary self telling him is the opposite of what it seems to say. After more than fifty years of study, he was still an ignoramus. The modern way of describing this is to say that Adams psychoanalyzes his soul to determine what it feels or what it means. After all, the therapeutic experience is essentially a literary one: A person is expected to think, reconstruct, maneuver—narrate with shape and interest—his old self to a listening doctor/auditor. A rich imagination is as useful as a sharp memory. Only when this old self is fully understood, in all its complexities and contradictions, the theory goes, can the patient be deemed healthy.

Adams would have described Franklin's life as wrong-headed, for he desires an inner search, not an outward pursuit. Franklin fixed on success, from the Latin *succedere*—ascending, mounting. As a failure, Adams had plummeted—into himself. He realizes how he must climb back out, and he presents it in the most curious turn taken in *The Education*. He decides to trace the history of force and power from the Middle Ages to the beginning of the twentieth century. In the midst of writing his autobiography he tells us that he must take up writing! Not only has self spawned self, but text has given rise to another, inner text. If the self is a reflexive phenomenon, and its history can be unraveled in writing, then why not a reflexive text as well. These intricacies—self doubling back on self, text on text, first person talking as third—make it appear as if the Book of Kells had provided the pattern for Adams's autobiography. In Adams's words: "In such labyrinths, the staff is a force almost more necessary than the legs; the pen becomes a sort of blind-man's dog, to keep him from falling into the gutters. The pen works for itself, and acts like a hand, modelling the plastic materials over and over again to the form that suits it best. The form is never arbitrary, but is a sort of growth like crystallization, as any artist knows too well; for often the pencil or the pen runs into side-paths and shapelessness, loses its relations, stops or is bogged. Then it has to return on its trail, and recover, if it can, its line of force. The result of a year's work depends more on what is struck out than on what is left in; on the sequence of the main lines of thought, than on their play or variety."

A chief obstacle to writing a modern autobiography is its ending. How can it end, really, reach its final conclusion, until the writer is dead? Franklin's *Autobiography* breaks off in his fifty-first year; he dies before its completion. Adams solves the problem by killing off the young Adams, the instructor. Or, perhaps in a more accurate literary image, the two Adamses come together, both holding a single pen. So the end of *The Education* is in some sense the birth of the Old Adams, complete with a new self.

After incorporating the idea of force into his writing by developing what he calls the Dynamic Theory of History, he arrives at the last chapter, appropriately titled "Nunc Age," (Now Go). He is ready to reenter the world. But before he does, he pauses to realize that he had accomplished the goal he set for himself in the Preface (which Adams signs as Henry Cabot Lodge): to complete Augustine's *Confessions*. Self-satisfied, Adams no longer needs to talk to himself. He can finally confess, quoting Shakespeare but recalling Augustine, that "the rest is silence."

VI. Untruth
and Narration

Both literary and moral feigning depend on the author's ability to reshape (in Latin fingere, *whence "fiction") his own thoughts of untruth, which in the late Middle Ages is called narration. Only when I have gotten used to thinking as the silent tracing of words on the parchment of my memory, can I detach thought from speech and contra-dict it. A full-blown lie presupposes a self that thinks before it says what it has thought. Only when memory is perceived as a text can thought become a material to be shaped, reshaped, and transformed. Only a self that has thought what it does say, can say something that it does not think. Neither such a thought as distinct from speech, nor such a thinking self as distinct from the speaker can exist without speech having been transmogrified and frozen into thought that is stored in the literate memory.*

IKE THE TEXT, Untruth also has a history. The Old Testament knows of infidelity, broken promises, betrayals, and perjury. It knows of slander, false witness and, what is worse, false prophecy and the abominable service of false gods. Neither these detestable forms of deceit nor the skillful ruse of a patriarch imply that opposition to an abstract "truth" that is essential to what we today call a lie. Neither the Greek *psuedos* (used both for the "liar" and the "lie") nor the Latin *mendacium* (referring also to the emendation of a line on a wax tablet) in Classical times comes close to our idea of the untruthful. Both languages lack the words that could oppose the *Oxford English Dictionary*'s "false statement made with the intent to deceive" to a flight of fancy or feigning. The Classical languages barely contain the seed for the full-fledged Western lie and the full-blown Western fiction.

The early Greeks took a sporting attitude toward duplicity. George Steiner presents an exchange between Athena and Odysseus as an example: ". . . mutual deception, the swift saying of 'things that are not,' need be neither evil nor a bare technical constraint. Gods and chosen mortals can be virtuosos of mendacity, contrivers of elaborate untruths for the sake of the verbal craft. . . ." And "untruth" is always the telling of *things* that are not, not of *thoughts* that are contradicted! The patron of this cunning craft was Hermes, the trickster, the thief and the inventor of the lyre that urges the singer further into the epos. And the hero of that art is the shrewd and wily, generous and noble Odysseus, who according to Plato (*Hippias Minor*) is powerful and prudent, knowing and wise in those things about which he is false.

In the realm of orality one cannot dip twice into the same wave, and therefore the lie is a stranger. My word always travels alongside yours; I stand for my word, and I swear by it. My oath is my truth until well into the twelfth century: The oath puts an end to any case against a freeman. Only in the thirteenth century does Continental canon law make the judge into a reader of the accused man's conscience, an inquisitor into truth, and torture the means by which the confession of truth is extracted from the accused. Truth ceases to be displayed in surface action and is now perceived as the outward expression of inner meaning accessible only to the self.

A B C

In the fifth century Augustine had created a concept that breaks with pagan and Christian antiquity by defining every lie as an assault on truth. Intellectual errors of fact are not a moral issue for him in his treatise *On the Lie*. Only the person who says something with the intent of misleading violates the truth. The offense lies in the *voluntas fallendi*: words used with the intent to contradict the truth that is enshrined in the speaker's heart. Even a statement that is factually correct can turn into an assault on truth if it is proffered with the intent to deceive. Augustine moved the lie into the neighborhood of blasphemy: an act of contempt of God as the only Creator and Author.

For the next eight hundred years whatever truly exists is there because God has willed it to be. All things man can speak about issue from His creative Word or command. He has brought things into being because He wanted them to be and not because there is something in them that makes it necessary for them to exist. Adam is His "fiction." He molded, shaped, fashioned him out of the virgin soil of Paradise. The world is therefore *contingent* on God's authorship. By every lie a creature usurps authorship reserved to the Creator. Even in the thirteenth century, a cleric who writes down stories has to state that he is not the story's actual source (*fons ejus*), but only its channel (*canalis*). Likewise, the person who had dictated the story to the scribe must state that he has not "sucked it from his finger" (*ex suo digito suxit*)—that is, has not *invented* it. The dictator's disclaimer lays bare the connection between fiction and *fingere*.

Augustine's ban on the arrogation of truth matured, during the Middle Ages, into the new duty to make truth manifest. In the many-tiered, God-willed order of the twelfth century, to be true in word and in deed came to be perceived as a moral debt. The late patristic prohibition against deceiving the listener was turned by the early Scholastics into the moral obligation to reveal the truth. Only against this background can it be understood what it means to say that the Age of European Literacy is the World of Fiction.

As much as the full-fledged lie, *narratio* presupposes an author and a text that is contingent on his self—his or her creation. Neither the epic bard, nor the later storyteller, nor even the highly literate poet are fully authors: They do not pretend to create a world that by the standards of the early Middle Ages would be untrue. Chaucer, Defoe, and Twain provide us with landmarks in the history of the author who weaves "lies" into the convincing untruth of fiction.

Chaucer, in *The Canterbury Tales* (1386), is the first English author who recognizes the emerging literate mindset of his courtly audience. Defoe, in the *Journal of the Plague Year* (1772), takes into account that the mind of his middle-class readership has been shaped by journals and magazines, and writes the first English "novel." And Twain publishes the first great work of fiction from Democratic America, *The Adventures of Huckleberry Finn*, in 1885, just two years after the *New England Journal of Education* had coined that curious Americanism, "literacy."

Modern readers take for granted that *The Canterbury Tales* is a standard book; after all, it is neatly printed and housed between solid boards. Moreover, its pages are filled with stories—eccentric characters involved in dramatic action. And that is, of course, exactly proper activity for books that are intended to be held in our hands and read to ourselves. But medievalists have been compiling convincing textual evidence since the mid thirties to prove that, while Chaucer's poem was written down by a number of scribes, it was in all likelihood delivered orally.

Which means that Chaucer's audience was prepared to listen to a long poem, presumably something they had done many times before. The majority of them, in fact, could probably not have read the poem, even if they so desired. Strangely enough, however, the opening lines of *The Canterbury Tales* demand a sophisticated literacy. Chaucer begins his poem with one of the most difficult syntactic forms for the listener to grasp, the subordinate clause, which requires the listener to hold the sense of the dependent clause steadily in mind, suspending the fulfillment of meaning that the independent clause promises to deliver. Chaucer compounds this highly literate construction—one that never appears in oral formulaic poetry—by beginning "The General Prologue" to *The Canterbury Tales* with not one but two consecutive subordinate clauses: the first from lines one to four, the second from lines five through eleven. He holds back the independent clause, "Thanne longen folk to goon on pilgrimages"—and hence leaves dangling the meaning of the early part of the poem—until line twelve.

By line twelve, however, Chaucer's audience would probably have forgotten what came before, or at best retained only a vague sense of it. His audience could only have felt uncomfortable, perhaps even irritated. To use a medieval designation, he has made them feel like *ignoramuses*. It is one thing to recite a poem using oral devices—formulaic constructions, repetitions—so that the audience can keep abreast and understand, but quite another to present the same information through highly literate techniques—in Chaucer's case, by using two sets of subordinate clauses and so forcing his audience to forget. By causing his audience to forget, however, Chaucer introduces one of the major concerns of the poem: the imposition of literacy upon an inherently oral activity— the composition and delivery of poetry.

If forgetting enables Chaucer to turn his audience into auditor/readers—in a sense, they must envision the page as they hear it aloud—it enables him to turn from storyteller into writer. And so he also points to his own ability to forget. Chaucer the narrator begins by telling us what he remembers about some thirty-three pilgrims with whom he sat one evening at the Tabard Inn and with whom he set out on the road to Canterbury. What is more astonishing, he intends to tell us, before he forgets it all, the four stories those pilgrims told on their round trip, "as it remembreth me," in the distinct voice of each of the pilgrims, utilizing their exact metaphor, image, color of language, and idea. All told, Chaucer will re-tell this entire event in over eighteen thousand lines, for the most part meticulously rhymed and metered—certainly a prodigious feat.

Prodigious or not, Chaucer employed this strategy knowing that his medieval audience would have believed him—but only up to a point. Indeed, if, as historians argue, Chaucer was probably educated at the Inns of Court, he would have learned some mnemonic system—his own Man of Laws learns "every statute . . . plein by rote"—and so would have been able to retell from memory a large amount of detail. But this is not Homer's Mnemosyne, that great treasure bag of phrases and images, into which one could dip, threading now one and now another on his marvelous loom. Chaucer's is a literate memory; many of the stories have been "sucked from his finger." And he boasts of remembering such minutiae that an audience—medieval or modern—is forced to conclude that he must be lying to them. No one could possibly remember that much detail with that much precision—mnemonic devices or not. As auditors, then, they would have been pulled up short.

Thus Chaucer deliberately undercuts his own demands for believability by presenting a new textual memory. No other writer—not Dante, or Gower, or Boccaccio—had used memory as such a storehouse for fiction. His audience would have been alert to a ploy, for in Chaucer they found such a revolutionary form. In a deliberate way, then, Chaucer focuses his audience's attention, not on his memory, but on forgetting.

Chaucer is composing his poem at a time when England is making its transition from an oral to a literate culture. And the poem reflects this uneasy shift. Chaucer presents us with details that he says he has overheard; but by the end of the fourteenth century, hearsay, at least in courts of law, was already being supplanted by written testimony. So while Chaucer roots his poem in oral tradition, he does so in such an overblown way that few if any of his contemporary listeners could have taken his boast seriously. Chaucer's strategy is simply to push the limits of orality to absurdity. He forces his medieval audience to hear *The Canterbury Tales* as a work of *literature*.

By getting them to think about their own literacy, as well as their own connections with the oral tradition, he has brought them face to face with the process of writing fiction. For if Chaucer could not possibly have remembered all that he says he has, he must be making it up, embellishing and shaping his initial information. He must be telling a story, inventing a tale. That is, he must be writing fiction. Chaucer is forging a working definition of the medieval idea of *auctor*, which he must of absolute necessity separate from the divine *auctoritee*. By assigning to himself the capacity to remember every scrap and nuance, every blink and titter of all thirty-three pilgrims, he sets himself up as a liar: a teller who intends to deceive with fibs and fables. Only by placing himself in this category can he become a mundane author. In any other category of literary creation, Chaucer would be usurping divine authorship.

Chaucer here becomes entangled in an important philosophical/theological idea of the Middle Ages—the question of "contingency." From Augustine to the end of the thirteenth century, the principle of contingency became the necessary cause for all creation. Contingency represents the state of an essence or nature that admits of, but does not demand, actualization. St. Thomas translated the idea to mean "that which can be and can not be," which he used as the basis for the demonstration of the existence of God. Since the essence of the contingent being does not itself contain its existence, the reason for its existence must be found in an extrinsic efficient cause. Antecedent causes must, likewise, find the reason for *their* existence in some other antecedent cause. Ultimately, the argument goes, one reaches a first cause whose existence is underived—that is, whose essence includes existence. But only one thing is both necessary and absolute: God.

This theological idea impinges on literary creation: The Canterbury pilgrims are dependent on Chaucer for their "existence"; he appears to be their absolute and necessary cause—though of course Chaucer's own existence is a contingent one. Still, the question arises: Is it proper in this fuzzy literary area to call Chaucer a creator? Literary creations must be seen, at least in part, as mirror images of heavenly creation. Chaucer falls into a literary trap: If the existence of the world is contingent on the grace of the Word in "divine authorship," then Chaucer can only escape blasphemy by undercutting that singular, tremendous power that enables him to create—literacy.

Chaucer's task is thus a complicated one. He needs to have his Canterbury story taken as truth—for this is the way readers come to enter into any fictional dream. He gains this sense of verisimilitude in several ways. By making himself one of the traveling group of pilgrims, Chaucer has to tell one of the proposed hundred and thirty or so tales, "The Tale of Sir Thopas," which he uses to further undercut his own literate power by telling a story so dull that the hosts beg him to stop. He adds even more of a sense of realism by drawing some of the other pilgrims—Harry Bailly the Host, for example—from actual citizenry of fourteenth-century London. Finally, there is no better way to imply that all this stuff is real than to say, "I was there, and I remember. I saw all this, I heard them all speak, and let me tell you what they said and did."

But while he needs to give his poem a sense of realism, for theological reasons he must also see to it that his audience experiences the poem as made up. It is inevitable, then, that the subject of his poem should be—at least in part—the paradoxical nature of literacy. The written word is the authorized version, the authenticated truth. But too much truth can get Chaucer into theological trouble; he must move his creation into another category, into untruth. And he can do this best by letting his audience think of him as a liar. And so the muse for Chaucer can no longer be Mnemosyne, the Goddess of Recollecting, but some other unnamed Goddess—of Forgetting.

Fiction reaches its first flowering in the *novel*—a word used initially to stand in opposition to the stuff of romances— when literacy broadened to include more of the middle class of English society in the late eighteenth century. The first successful London daily newspaper, the *Daily Courant*, appeared March 11, 1702. The word *magazine* was first used to designate a popular literary journal with the publication of the *Gentleman's Magazine* in 1704. In this context, the most literate genre, the novel, begins to take shape through the efforts of Daniel Defoe, a man who in 1704 printed his own weekly newspaper, the *Review*. His *Journal of the Plague Year* is usually referred to as England's first novel.

Like Chaucer, Defoe needs to establish the veracity of a new form. While Defoe's audience may be more used to reading than Chaucer's, and, in particular, used to reading fictional narratives like romances, the novel is, as its name implies, *new*. Like Chaucer, Defoe wants his story to be taken as true, and so he needs to fabricate a believable lie, which he does by presenting his narrative as a journal kept by one H. F., who purportedly lived during the plague year of 1665. This H. F. gives an eye- and ear-witness account; in fact, the subtitle of the book reads: "Being observations or memorials of the most remarkable occurences, as well publik as private, which happened in London during the last great visitation in 1665. Written by a citizen who continued all the while in London. Never made publik before." Thus, H. F.'s account derives from what he saw (observations) and remembers (memorials), all of which, he assures us, is true (happened in London).

Defoe's premise differs from Chaucer's in that the former admits to writing down events daily in a journal and finally making the journal public—that is, publishing his evidence. Between Chaucer and Defoe the printing press has intervened, and it turns out that Defoe's real subject is the bureaucratization of the word, authenticated through the reality of type, and spread like contagion, in hundreds and hundreds of copies, directly from the platen of the press. The printed word impresses its own version of reality.

Defoe opens his journal by conjecturing on the origin of the plague, surprised that it might have come from Holland, but suggesting that no one really knows, since "we had no such thing as printed newspapers in those days to spread rumors and reports of things. . . ." News traveled by "word of mouth," but the truth of the plague cannot be gotten in that manner. In time, however, as the *Journal* makes clear, the Secretaries of State "got knowledge of it," and took on the responsibility of determining the truth and making it known to the citizens—a bureaucratic process that will reach its final goal in publication.

First, the State sends out professionals, two physicians and a surgeon, as certified agents, to examine the corpses of two recently dead Frenchmen. Through an undisclosed procedure, they determine that the Frenchmen both died of the plague. They render their opinion to the parish clerk, who turns over their positive findings to city hall. The last step toward truth involves making public—publishing—the doctors' decisions in the weeky Bill of Mortality: "Plague, 2. Parishes infected, 1." The plague has thus begun, its reality contained in the first Bill of Plague posted at various places around the parish. From this point on, no rumor, no piece of information transmitted orally can counter the truth of the written reports.

Few people dare question the physicians' verdicts, for these men are certified professionals. Their published reports become automatic testimony in the bureaucratization of the word. And their word helps create the reality of the plague; indeed, as the news travels by the Plague Bill, so does the infection, for people act on the printed reality. Spreading the plague by word of mouth, they close themselves in, huddling closer together, unwittingly serving to infect each other. "Facts" matter very little. The narrator of the *Journal* actually sees very few dead bodies; he merely reprints the body counts from the weekly Plague Bill. The citizens of London learn that the plague is getting worse or getting better by the numbers of people reported in the weekly Bill. The reality of the plague resides in these figures; the shadow of the medical "truth" of the plague lies somewhere else—in rats or in fleas, or in some other theory. But these "medical facts" interest no one but the historian of disease, or the medical scientist.

Defoe's narrative account mimics this social construction of the plague. Defoe himself was four years old during the plague—hardly an eye- or ear-witness. That doesn't matter. For he knows he is free to make up the facts, or at least to play with them, keeping only the barest remnant of historical accuracy and molding the rest to fit his aesthetic needs. Defoe invents events, plays with statistics. Compare Defoe's account with other "historical" accounts of the plague and the numbers all differ. Knowing that he is writing both fiction and history, Defoe can call into question the notion of truth.

His literary task is in some ways more difficult, in some ways easier, than Chaucer's. He knows, for instance, that people firmly believe in the veracity of the *news*—as it is presented in the dailies, in magazines, or now in novels. (Both *news* and *novel* thrive on the freshness of the word; each ultimately derives from Latin *nova*, "new.") It is in this period that the idea of story begins to separate itself from history: What constitutes "untruth" and "fact" take separate paths. And *news* helps forge that separation. Defoe takes advantage of this confusion between story and history: in his own story, he shows us that what people lose faith in are forms of oral discourse. Old wives' tales, rumors, forecasts by astrologers—all of these are stuff, Defoe alleges, of the deluded minds of the common people in eighteenth-century London. Some of these illiterates, Defoe tells us, were even silly enough to run "about the streets with their oral predictions," publishing them as best they could. But he is reporting all of this, of course, in a skillfully made-up work of *fiction*. Thus, like Chaucer, he undercuts a growing reliance on literate forms—testimony, records, numbers—with a literate form, the novel.

In the *Journal*, literacy impresses itself more and more deeply into the text, crowding out virtually every oral locution. In the early part of the *Journal*, Defoe uses phrases like "it was about the beginning of September, 1664," "some said," "pretty much," "about six weeks," "others said it was brought from Canada; others from Cyprus." These terms of vague approximation are slowly extinguished and replaced by precise numbers. The supposition, of course, is that numbers carry accuracy, precision, and hence the truth. These are things we can believe in and act on.

Gradually, as we read the *Journal*, we begin to realize that we are being infected—or rather that Defoe's *Journal*, his attempt at establishing the scientific veracity of the plague, is infecting us. He makes us believe, with his reportorial, exact mind, that "oral discourse" does not have the capacity for carrying the truth; oral discourse does not allow for the power of critical analysis. For that, one must have writing, or better yet, the authority of print. One must be able to "think" about the problem through discursive prose. The sentences must stand still, an impossibility with oral discourse. Those who remain outside this literate circle will thus remain incapable of thinking.

Prose is not democratic. Not everyone can read. But neither is the plague—Defoe tells us that it affects the poor in greater numbers than the wealthy. The irony of this book begins to become apparent. While the majority of Londoners will survive the plague, they will not survive the new literacy. For the plague, this crisis of the State, has been met with the best weapon the State has at its disposal: certification through the word. Through it, in fact, the State has managed to concentrate, solidify, and expand its power. It is one thing to create civil servants, but an entirely other thing both to invest them with power and to coerce the population to believe in that power.

But we must once again understand the literary trick: Defoe makes his readers fall for the power of the printed word. He not only says he was there—so were a lot of other people—but he wrote all this down. And that is why he now stands in the privileged position of passing on the truth. Where Chaucer was careful to work out a limited sense of his own power as an author, walking a fine line with the ultimate authorial power, Defoe has already assumed the power of the word to create his own historical fabrication with it. But we should note that, as with Chaucer, the trick is two-edged. For at the same time that he establishes the validity of the word, he also distrusts it, and so undercuts it by associating it metaphorically with the plague. This might have been more apparent for an eighteenth-century reader than for a modern one, far removed from the event of the plague. By 1667, there were at least a dozen contemporary accounts of the plague, including the authoritative eight-volume *Loimologia sine pestis nuperae apud populum londinensem narratio* by Quincey, published in 1720. And Defoe's facts and figures are at best shaky. Not because he is a sloppy historian, but because he understands the true nature of history: That it is a narrative in the best sense of the word and that the "facts" must therefore be constructed.

In *The Adventures of Huckleberry Finn*, Mark Twain lays for his readers the nineteenth-century equivalent of this trap of literacy. At the same time that literacy opens the lid a crack to the treasure trove of white, received society—one that is, of course, closed to the Negro Jim—it also exacts a high price, and so Huck flees it.

Huckleberry Finn is a book about a book. And we won't know about the literary character Huck, Huck himself tells us in the opening line, "without you have read a book by the name of *The Adventures of Tom Sawyer*." Here is a literary creation telling us to read about his past in another book—the genealogy of the Homeric epic transformed into literary

pedigree. We have come a long way: Twain achieves his verisimilitude by coming clean, by laying bare the literary lie—
this is only a book, these are only characters playing out their
parts. Having established Huck's literary credentials, Twain
has Huck follow what is now a familiar pattern: He undercuts
that literary importance. "But that aint no *matter*," Huck insists, immediately after telling us to read *Tom Sawyer*, pulling
off a wonderfully literate pun. It doesn't make any difference
is one sense of Huck's line; but it can also mean that books
are without substance, *materia*—without matter.

Huck probably means both things. But we must be more
on guard with Twain than with any other author, for he is so
disarmingly honest—or rather, his confederate, Huck, tells
us his creator is so honest. He's so honest, in fact, Huck con-
fesses, that in his other books "Mister Twain told us the truth,
mainly. There was things which he stretched, but mainly he
told the truth."

Standing inside a formal literary tradition, this semiliterate
begins his story by telling about his early days with the Widow
Douglas and her sister, Miss Watson, who both set out to
civilize Huck by teaching him the rules. They do it principally
by reading to him from Miss Watson's book about "Moses
and the bulrushers." When this fails to impress its mark on
Huck, Miss Watson escalates to a spelling book.

In this emerging world of literacy, correct spelling offers
the key to the correct look of literacy, the visual check on a
person's education, in much the same way that skin color is a
key in this book to freedom or slavery. A person usually knows
enough grammar to sound literate; and speech betrays no errors of punctuation or spelling, only mispronunciations. So,
for example, Huck speaks the word *civilization*, but in writing

the book he spells it *sivilization*. In the twelfth century, Huck would have been classed as a *rustico more*, someone who communicates in an unlearned tongue for which there exists no written counterpart bound by grammatical rules.

Huck's misspellings are common to the illiterate, who pay more attention to what they hear, without recognizing on the page the words they frequently use. We know what Huck means, but that "aint no matter." And here we step into the first part of Twain's trap. What Huck says takes a secondary position to the *way* Huck presents—"writes"—it. Anyone who is able to read *Huck Finn* is obviously literate, literate enough to harbor the impulse to correct Huck's mistakes, for the mistakes loom as boulders impeding the smooth and steady flow of the reader's fluency. To borrow the central image of the book: We need to transform Huck's babbling stream of speech into a smooth flowing river of prose.

This book forces us to read in an aristocratic way, in a modern obverse of Hugh of Saint Victor's, in which the critic, the inner self that sits in judgement, silently corrects Huck's speech. This is not the reading of contemplative silence, but the busy-ness of critical judging. Twain has made us not only into readers, but editors; and our laughter at Huck's mannerisms must sound haughty—in the sense of high and lofty—as we elevate ourselves over that poor, unlettered boy. Twain provokes that judgement in part because the book seems to be a reproduction of the spoken and not the written word. In precisely the manner that a medieval scribe recorded what he heard in *ductus*, Twain creates the illusion that Huck dictated this novel and that what we have as a result is a raw medieval manuscript, which we read out of literate training as modern critics. After all our years of education about and knowledge of the rules of grammar and syntax and spelling, we simply cannot allow him his sloppy freedom. We need to correct him, keep him in check—even against our wills—as strongly as the Widow Douglas and Miss Watson.

Twain makes us feel superior to Huck's mistakes. Even though he speaks—and even though he tells us that he has written this book—we can only conclude that he is dumb. In early use, in Old High German, the word *dumb* meant one who was both mute *and* stupid. Perhaps the logic went something like this: Because we don't hear what the person knows or understands, we assume he knows nothing. Only saints and sages are assumed in their silence to be wise. In Huck's case, we assume he is dumb precisely because we *see*, *verbum ad verbum*, what he is *saying*. In a poignant way, he has been "silenced" by prose. His words have undergone no *re*-vision. He says what he thinks at first glance. And since his story is not, in a traditional sense, authored, what he writes cannot be taken as authority. Even in nineteenth-century society, he might as well be mute. For in his illiterate ignorance, he is as disenfranchised from society as his Negro friend Jim.

Twain drives home just how strongly we are chained to our own literacy through Huck's illiterate silence. While he allows Huck to live comfortably in orality, he prevents us from entering that world. *The Canterbury Tales* begs to be read aloud—one can hear it in the easy rhythms of "The General Prologue" and in Chaucer's hilarious rhymes, for instance when he undercuts the romantic *kisse* in "The Miller's Tale" with the earthy *pisse*. It may not matter if Defoe's *Journal* is read aloud or not. A journal is a fairly private affair, but one can easily imagine it read aloud to a group of close friends. At any rate, Defoe's subject is a public one.

A B C

There is no question about the way *The Adventures of Huckleberry Finn* must be read. If the book is not read silently on the page, it loses its meaning. Huck's illiterate phonetic prose ties us to our own literacy. For if we want to get all of the humor Twain intends, we must *see* Huck's sentences and not *hear* them. For example, when we read Huck's *sivilization* aloud, we miss the irony of the mistake. If Twain makes Huck dumb, then he makes us mute.

Twain shocks us with his anachronistic linguistics: He would have us think that there is only one language—the spoken one that through writing or printing is made visible on the page. And he has pulled this illiterate kid out of the woods to embody this irony, twenty years after the War for Emancipation—that is, the struggle for wholesale American democracy. It is ironic, for, of course, there are two languages—the one that we freely speak and the one, orthographically and grammatically correct, that appears on the printed page. And they are radically different in what they convey. We might expect Huck's brand of speaking from someone like Jim, not yet fully integrated into the educational scheme, but certainly not from Huck, a young white adolescent. He should know better; and Twain forces us, the literate readers, to teach him. To use Hugh of Saint Victor once more as an example, it is as if his comment—*per se inspectiones*—had become a curse, transforming forever speech into words never to fly free from the text again.

A text imprisoned in the page also cannot be successfully translated. Huck's idiom and jargon, his mispronunciations and misspellings will not convert in any way to another language. So Twain's text is frozen fast. The second part of Twain's trap snaps on this idea. We may feel smug about correcting that dumb kid's spelling, or dismissing Jim's spells. But in his loose and sloppy jargon, that dumb boy has given us one of the greatest novels in America. This may be the boldest lie in all of American fiction. Huck has created something grander than most of his readers are capable of doing—in their educated prose. God knows what Jim is capable of doing. Aren't we all, Twain may be asking, the ones enslaved by our mannered language, ordered and ruled and in which it may be more difficult to write about freedom and the great meandering Mississippi than in Huck's dialect?

Twain asks for a broad reading of slavery. For Huck is just as removed, just as cut off from society as Jim. Jim is even more radically illiterate than Huck, but for him every inch of the world is animate—the weather, the fog, the river. His reality breathes strongly through superstition and spells; his knowledge is still gained from what lies around him. Tom Sawyer has developed his perceptions from reading Arthurian romances, and in the course of the novel he passes this on to Huck. Tom's solutions to problems are intricate and complicated, Jim's are immediate. When this book was written, slaves had already been granted their legal freedom; when the narrative begins, Jim has already been granted his by his owner. Twain lumps Huck and Jim together: they both appear to be fugitives; they float on the same raft; they are friends who speak the same sort of dialect. If Huck is stupid, then so is Jim. But if we can appreciate the language—and we do partly because we enjoy the book so much—then we must grant to Huck great brilliance, and we must allow that same possibility for Jim. In a sense, we must see them both as "articulate" human beings. We must grant them their freedom. By stepping into Twain's linguistic trap, we are forced into being abolitionists. We have to come to appreciate the richness and the power and the beauty of that oral culture—both black and white. Freed from rules and regulations, their language unites them: Huck and Jim learn from each other.

Civilization in this novel resides on the riverbanks—the world of Miss Polly and Widow Douglas and Judge Thatcher. The raft is an island of orality on which these two characters float along, separated from the land. Facts and details from the riverbank fade into metaphor and image on the raft. Like Chaucer and Defoe, Twain is struggling with the phenomenon of literacy. Chaucer adopts a fictional stance—his prodigious memory—that undercuts itself so that his audience can accept a made-up story. Defoe too presents us with a literate form—the journal—and then proceeds to undercut it by showing us that the plague exists in great part only in authorized descriptions on the page, and that perhaps the true victims are those unfortunates who remain illiterate, and who, as a result, will be left behind by the march of progress. In Twain, the process is more complicated, for by presenting us with an illiterate but brilliant character he forces his readers to undercut their *own* literacy.

Chaucer is still writing for an audience that is essentially illiterate. He is concerned with the coming of literacy, only to the extent that it forces him to confront what it means to write fiction. For Defoe, literacy is a perceptual problem: How does print affect the way people understand the world? For Twain, in nineteenth-century America, literacy is a problem of the highest political and social order. It gets at the heart of democratic America. Let us understand, he seems to say, that two languages mean two Americas—in terms of the novel, two classes: the Judge Thatchers and the Jims and the Hucks.

If we applaud Huck at the end of the novel, then we must also clap our hands for Jim. And if we allow Huck to light out for the territory at the end of the book, then we must set Jim free.

Thus, Twain brings into focus the trap of literacy. There is a whole world in *Huck Finn* that is closed to those without literacy. They can't, for ironic example, read this marvelous work, *The Adventures of Huckleberry Finn*. And yet we must recognize a world rich with superstition and folklore, with adventure and beauty, that remains closed to those who are too tightly chained to letters. But Twain forces us also to look forward, for by the end of the nineteenth century, very little territory remained. Only small pockets of orality still survive in the country—mostly rural, mostly poor, mostly black. The rest is literate in the most sweeping way. By 1885 the *New England Journal of Education* was already conducting surveys to determine levels of literacy in Cambridge, Massachusetts. No one would have thought in the nineteenth century that we would be hanging fast to literacy, as we see it too vanishing: People now becoming enslaved to the power of a machine in their pursuit of computer literacy. So long as we remain as aware as Twain, we have lost nothing.

VII. From Taught Mother Tongue to Newspeak and Uniquack

The language that we hear spoken today is full of words of a special type: These words we will call amoeba-words, and the vocabulary that they constitute, Uniquack. Amoeba-words all possess at least three fields of usage; let "energy" serve as an example of such a word. "Energy" has an initial meaning that is traditional. According to the Oxford English Dictionary, in 1599, it means "vigor of expression," and later the impressive capacity of an utterance or of organ music. The term energy is still widely used in this first sense of vigor. During the nineteenth century, energy also became a technical term. At first, it was used quite generally by physicists to denote the body's ability to perform work. Then, precisely at the same time that Marx ascribed "labor force" to the proletariat, several German physicists ascribed to Nature a general potential to perform work, and called it "energy." For the last hundred years, the term has been used in physics to verbalize an increasingly abstract alternative energy, or energy needs. We must be forever conscious of the fact that we do not know what those terms mean. We use the words like words from Scripture, like a gift from above. Furthermore, we gratefully transfer the power to define their meaning to an expertocratic hierarchy to which we do not belong. The word "energy" in this context is used neither with common sense, nor with the senseless precision of science, but almost like a sublinguistic grunt—a nonsense word. Energy, like sexuality, transportation, education, communication, information, crisis, problem, solution, role, and dozens of other words, belong, in this sense, to the same class.

HEN ORWELL wrote about Newspeak, no computer language had as yet been named or published. Our theme therefore will not be computer language, but Orwell's attempt to caricature what happens when speakers of ordinary language treat it as if it can be reduced to a code. This perception of Newspeak is not made by Orwell, of course, but by a pair of latecomers, who see the unfolding of a cipher Orwell created over thirty-five years ago.

Newspeak and Uniquack are two-egged twins. In the fifties, when the computer was a novelty and UNIVAC the trade name of the only machine that could be purchased, James Reston created Uniquack in an editorial aside. We adopted the term Uniquack for the jelly formed of amoeba-words, words that are neither "significant and binding for certain activities" nor "indicative of certain forms of thought"— the two characteristics that together determine Raymond Williams' choice of Key-Words, although like Williams' Key-Words, amoeba-words are often strong and difficult and persuasive in everyday language, and serve to indicate wider areas of experience. As the years went by, Newspeak and Uniquack became useful to name two characteristics that make late twentieth-century, everyday English, French, or German, alike and distinct from ordinary languages in former times.

Newspeak is a transparent neologism. For Orwell, it is the fictional portrait of the deliberate distortion of an Oldspeak that never was. In this age of computers, which Orwell did not live to see, his Newspeak is an ominous parody of the intent to use English as a "medium of communication." This tendency is fostered by the spread of Uniquack: the degradation that results from the fallout of scientific discourse into ordinary speech. Newspeak thus refers—in our usage—pri-

ABC

marily to an attitude of the speaker toward what he does, while
Uniquack refers to the predominance of a special kind of vocabulary in his speech. By using the two terms in conjunction
when speaking about certain features of contemporary language, we hope to escape the objections that literal-minded
professors have raised repeatedly against Orwell: Namely,
that we engage in shallow and uncritical linguistics. It is not
our intention to oppose a paranoiac vision of today's communication to the romantic utopia of a virgin vernacular that
mirrors a factual truth.

Newspeak and Uniquack are neologisms of very different
status. As a foundling, Uniquack can be adopted to our purposes. Newspeak is well-worn. Orwell conceived it as a caricature of his own abandoned belief in a world language and
used it as a literary device to make a fable stick. Since his
death, it has become the label for a muddled complex of be-
liefs. Today, it is mostly used to promote the nonsensical belief
that language has become useless.

Orwell used the term on two different levels—as a parody
and as an element of his world of 1984. The two main sources
for his linguistic parody are Basic English, proposed by Ogden, and Interglossa, conceived by Hogben—both of which
had their heyday in the early thirties. Both are attempts to
create a world language based on English and containing less
than 850 words. In 1939, Ezra Pound praised Basic as "a
magnificent system for measuring extant works . . . an instrument for the diffusion of ideas . . . with advantages . . .
obvious to any man of intelligence." In the 1940s no less a
person than William Empson praised Basic as an instrument
to understand poetry and as a vocabulary for pithy poetic creation. Winston Churchill had the British government pur-

chase the copyright to Basic. And H. G. Wells, in *The Shape of Things to Come*, pictures a utopia in which the rapid diffusion of Basic as the *lingua franca* of the world is "one of the un-anticipated achievements of the twenty-first century."

Orwell describes the world that Wells saw coming as a "vision of humanity, liberated by the machine, a race of enlightened sunbathers, whose sole topic of conversation is their own superiority to their ancestors." If he too had once believed in Basic, his parody of it is part of Orwell's lampoon, as Wells describes it, of a "glittering, strangely sinister world, in which the privileged classes live a life of shallow, gutless hedonism, and the workers . . . toil like troglodytes in caverns underground."

The satirical force with which Orwell used Newspeak to serve as his portrait of one of those totalitarian ideas that he saw taking root in the minds of intellectuals everywhere can be understood only if we remember that he speaks with shame about a belief that he formerly held. Just as he had to go to Spain, to Catalonia, to be disabused of his left-wing do-goodism, he had to join the BBC to promote Basic before he understood that it could only be used as a deadly, mechanical substitute for thought.

From 1942 to 1944, working as a colleague of William Empson's, he produced a series of broadcasts to India written in Basic English, trying to use its programmed simplicity, as a *Tribune* article put it, "as a sort of corrective to the oratory of statesmen and publicists." Only during the last year of the war did he write "Politics and the English Language," insisting that the "defense of the English language has nothing to do with the setting up of a Standard English."

Basic is an ultimate effort to standardize speech according

A B C

to a written model: To put "language," which has come into existence by recording speech sounds through the alphabet, and which then has been corrected by the grammarian, back into the mouths of the people in this new form. The attempt to make people use this artifact whenever they speak has a history. At this point, it seems helpful to look back at this origin. Orwell stumbled on the title for his novel by reversing the date, 1948, when he had completed writing. Taking an Orwellian liberty with 1942, the year that Orwell began broadcasting Basic English on the BBC, we arrive at 1492, the year that Nebrija suggested to the Spanish royalty that they might control their subjects through the use of a taught mother tongue. Six years before the publication of *1984*, Orwell found a descendent of Nebrija's monster in Ogden's Basic English, which he could broadcast through the BBC. The image is one of Orwell setting sail for the Brave New World. Finally, he dropped Basic for its parody in Newspeak. From Nebrija to Orwell: From Spaniards who would speak taught mother tongue, to Proles who are tongue-tied.

In this movement from the parody of Basic English to the parable of the speechless horror of meaningless utterances, Orwell reveals a new dimension in writings on the future. Orwell was steeped in the genre of utopian literature; from his own statements, it is clear that he was well aware of the place that utopian writers had assigned to language. Swift has the people of Laputa fed by their "political projectors" with "invented, simplified language, [who] write books by machines and educate their pupils by inscribing the lesson on wafers . . . causing them to swallow it." In the year that he left the BBC, Orwell comments that the "one aim of intellectual totalitarianism cannot but be to make people less conscious."

Jack London, whose imagery surfaces frequently in *1984*, describes his "proles" (Orwell uses the same term) as "phrase-slaves" who consider the coinage of such utopian phrases as "an honest dollar" or "a full dinner pail" strokes of genius. London too has loudspeakers establish and anchor the regime. All the isolated elements out of which Orwell constructed the parable called Newspeak he took either from Ogden or the Utopians.

What is unique about Newspeak is the same thing that makes the whole of *1984* into a new kind of horror story. To quote Herbert Read: "*1984* is a Utopia in reverse: Not an *Erewhon*, which is utopia upside down. *Erewhon* is still written after the ameliorative pattern of utopia itself: You may paradoxically be punished for being ill, but the ideal is health. In *1984* the pattern is malevolent . . ." The malevolence of this pattern is implicit in the existing state and does not result from abuse or the self-serving manipulation by an elite. In Jack London's *Iron Heel*, as in Zamyatin's *Zero*, power is still a means; in *1984* the power implicit in the State is the ultimate reason for everything that happens. And the State has turned into a book that is constantly rewritten. Power is no longer at the service of the elite; the elite itself is at the service of power, which is a book. The worst that H. G. Wells could imagine was inequality—albeit a monstrous kind. According to Orwell, Wells "was too sane to understand the modern world."

Orwell's predecessors who wrote upside-down utopias invented horrible abuses of language. Orwell describes communication that takes place after the extinction of language itself. Newspeak is not the language of dystopia, but of the speechless utterances of Kakitopia 1984. Orwell created the parable of human beings compelled to communicate—

mostly through organized hatred—and to do so without human language.

Literary critics and those who use Newspeak as an English word in ordinary conversation usually mean either the corrupt English of propagandists and the ambiguous language of politicians and broadcasters, or the neologisms coined by the adversary. In this imprecise fashion they imply terminological inflation, effective sloganeering, or the antonym of English before the Fall. Orwell's Newspeak, however, is something more sinister than the proliferating *idiotikon* of technical terms that make conversations in the real 1984, and after, so "noisy." We see Newspeak as a cipher for something that is now called "interpersonal communication," for the belief that the terms by which we describe the operations of computers are fit to tell what is going on between you and me. By Newspeak we mean one particular way of thinking and speaking about language—an approach or an attitude that treats language as a system and a code.

The equation between man and machine was not entirely unknown to Orwell. He knew Mary Shelley's *Frankenstein* (1816) and probably also T. H. Huxley's hypothesis that animals are automata (1874). But the new wave, according to which digital-analog computers meaningfully model human "brains" did not hit the press until Orwell was dead. As a novelist, he invented a parable for a scientific hypothesis that hovered in the air. He created the idea of communication without sense or meaning, before he could use the computer to model it on. O'Brian from the Thought Police says to Smith, whom he tortures: "we do not merely destroy our enemies, we change them . . . we convert, we shape them . . . We make our enemy one of ourselves before we kill him . . . make the brain perfect before we blow it out . . . the command of old despotisms was 'thou art' . . . what happens to you here is forever. . . ." Smith, the novel's antihero, still believes that what happens makes sense to O'Brian. He has to accept that O'Brian's world is senseless and that he must join O'Brian in this powerful nonsense. "There is learning, there is understanding, and there is acceptance. It is time for you [Smith] to enter upon the second stage . . . tell me, why we cling to power . . . speak." Strapped to the rack, Winston answers: "You are ruling over us for our own good." He gives the answer that would have satisfied Dostoyevski's Grand Inquisitor: "You believe that human beings are not fit to govern themselves and therefore. . . ." As his only response, O'Brian turns the lever to thirty-three degrees of torture. A pang of pain contorts Winston. And then O'Brian instructs Winston: "We seek power entirely for its own sake." And the State, which O'Brian represents, creates and recreates Winston's human nature, according to its own text, and allows Winston to exist only in the context of the State.

Today, we would say that O'Brian *programs* Winston for his *role* in *1984*. Orwell knew these two words only in their theatrical sense: The schedule of performance sold by an attendant, and the text studied by an actor. "To program" was first used in 1945 for the act of expressing an operation in the terms appropriate for the performance of a computer. And "role theory" was then a new trend in sociology. Neither word had fallen from its specialized orbit into ordinary speech to become amoeba-words. Turing's idea of an algorithm that adapts its state according to the outcome of its last calculation was well understood by Wiener and Neumann, who created a machine that made such a formula autonomous from human calculation, but the general public still saw in the computer nothing but a more perfect adding machine. The concept of "role" had been introduced in the same year as Turing's idea by independent publications of Margaret Mead, Ralph Linton, and Murdock, and by 1950 was considered basic to all sociology by Parsons and Merton; but its implied assumption that all social relations can be reduced to power or the interchange of information between individual role-players had certainly never occurred to George Orwell. And yet, as a novelist, he has O'Brian force Winston to become what role-theory and the cybernetic model of human communication assume as "human nature." Kakitopia fits these assumptions: "Power is (precisely) in tearing human minds to pieces and putting them together again in new shapes of your own choosing," O'Brian says to his pupil. Newspeak assumes the existence of plastic human individuals who can be written and rewritten into any role. Thus the Kakitopia of Newspeak, the exchange of communication between nonhuman entities, and the reduction of social action to mere exchanges became thinkable about the same time.

The proponents of a cybernetic model of social analysis assume that human beings fit their assumptions, but Orwell knows that to fit, each one has to accept what is done to him. And O'Brian knows that no one can perform this acceptance for you. Winston, who had worked in the Ministry of Truth, knew what Newspeak was. Under torture, he understood what nonhuman communication was: mere know-"how" without meaning or "why." O'Brian asked him to understand his message, not him, to abandon the urge to understand what he, the speaker, meant and to let his mind be dictated to—and to be nothing but the result of this dictation. The reduction of an encounter with another person into an exchange of information between two elements of a system—what we today call "system-theory"—Orwell called "collective solipsism."

Winston understood what O'Brian asked him to do, and he tried hard to do it: He learned to register how things were supposed to be and to spell them out without asking "why," but he did not accept being part of the system, not until he had gone through Room 101. Only there he accepts himself as part of "a fantasy world in which things happen as they should"—namely, on a blank page, that is, as dictation. And to accept being a part of this fantasy of pure senseless power, Winston had to erase his self. But no violence that he inflicted on himself could break his common sense—which Orwell often calls "decency." To turn himself into non-sense he has to betray his love. Not torture, but only self-betrayal could make him like O'Brian. In O'Brian's words, Winston's own acts are "the things from which you could not recover. Something is killed in your breast: burnt out, cauterized out." And this is what Winston does to himself when he has to face the rats in Room 101 and he begs his torturers: "Do it to Julia." This betrayal transformed his habit of Doublethink into a conditioned reflex. Later on, he and Julia meet again, as two burnt-out hulls, knowing that in Room 101 they had both meant what they had said. Self-betrayal was the last thing that Winston *meant*. By becoming the torturer of his last love, in his own mind Winston had become as self-less as O'Brian. Henceforth, the unique mutual intimacy between the executioner and the victim integrated both him and Julia into the system, the solipsism of meaningless communication.

What we are retelling and commenting on here is a fable,

not a mere parody of Esperanto, or a cautionary tale, or linguistic theory dressed up in metaphor. This fable shows a society that survives the radical renunciation of language on the part of its members. We shall not be seduced by Orwell's journalistic genius to take it as something that could happen, or that he himself thought could happen. Newspeak remains an "ideal type," a cipher for language that never could be because its speakers would be totally unlike the men and women we know. And yet, Newspeak has the power to evoke a strange sense of deja vu, because it is modeled not only on Basic English, which has never been spoken, but also on the language of science, which also stands for something that never could be.

When a physicist writes "E" on the blackboard, he proves himself one of the boys. He shows off his competence in using an algorithm, which over several generations, has incorporated all the rules according to which it may be put into a formula. When "E" is used this way, it has no meaning outside the context of theoretical physics. The physicist's ability to pronounce the written "E" as energy, however, is not the result of a conspiracy, but of careful training, part of which consists in keeping the formalism of theoretical physics apart from the meanings of ordinary life. The difference between the two has often been compared with bilingual existence; but this comparison fosters a mistake. Spoken English, Japanese, and Kwakiutl—all three are meaningful in everyday, sensual life. The so-called "language" of physics is a code, a system of signs, a formal theory, an analytic tool that derives part of its value from its near-independence from ordinary speech. A physicist limited to the use of his technical vocabulary would be totally speechless in a bedroom or kitchen, but his gibberish would not be Newspeak. The tour de force accomplished by Orwell consists in the invention of a malevolent conspiracy that imposes the use of that kind of code in everyday life. Paranoiac assumptions are essential to Orwell's cipher. If we were to call the language of physics a form of Newspeak, that would only frustrate our attempt to reserve this term as the name for an attitude toward ordinary speech.

There is, however, an important, indirect way by which the proliferation of special codes contributes to our growing tendency to speak at dinner as if we were in the psychology or sociology lab. We increasingly use ordinary words that have been picked up by one or several "codes" and to which technical meanings have been attached. And we tend to use them indiscriminately, giving the impression that their technical meaning is somehow connoted in our use of the term. While we mean to say "screw," we say "having sex" and we imply "sexuality," a scientific construct we had no intention of implying. Good strong words used in this technical way in ordinary speech generate a following of amoeba-words, which can be made to mean anything, like a mathematician's "E." And this fallout then fosters the attitude toward language that we have called Newspeak. These waste products from technical word-factories are akin to pollution. Just as the unintended by-products of industry have penetrated, reshaped, and degraded most anything that we see, touch, breathe, or eat, so have these waste products of terminologies affected ordinary language. Much of this terminological waste merely generates noise in everyday conversation and can be compared with the dull expanses of cement that economic growth has produced. But within this waste, many terms are potential amoeba, blown up with hot air, brandished, and loaded with ominous connotations, while losing all denotation. The prudent person who wishes to make sense is often forced to declare a moratorium on their use.

Again, we are speaking in terms that hardly could have been Orwell's. "Pollution" was as unknown to him as the vocabulary of the computer. Its meaning was "seminal emission apart from coition." The counterpurposive effects of technical decisions were not discussed in the forties. Rachel Carson had not yet published her *Silent Spring*. "Fallout" meant the deferred effects of the Hiroshima bomb, and not the exhaust from belching chimneys. Though he wrote an upside-down utopia, Orwell, like Wells or Huxley or Zamyatin, was still primarily concerned with the intentional misuse of the new powerful means. He went beyond these predecessors because, unlike them, he deciphered and lampooned a new logic inherent in the intellectual project that generated computer, bomb, role-theory. He explored the destructive implications of high-sounding ideals; his witches were intellectual do-gooders and their totalitarian projects. His originality lay in the parody of their intent. He was a prophet, in the Hebrew sense—one who sees clearly into the present—because he discovered the forties. He could not foresee that in the eighties so many people—without having passed through Room 101—would try to convince themselves that they "communicate"—and, in addition, mostly in Uniquack.

Postscript:
Silence and the We

George Steiner closes After Babel, *"in which the problem of Babel and of the nature of language is so insistently examined," with the statement that the Kabbalah "knows of a day of redemption on which translation will no longer be necessary. All human tongues will have re-entered the translucent immediacy of that primal, lost speech shared by God and Adam. . . . But the Kabbalah also knows of a more esoteric possibility. It records the conjecture, no doubt heretical, that there shall come a day when translation is not only unnecessary but inconceivable. Words will rebel against man. They will shake off the servitude of meaning. They will 'become only themselves, and as dead stones in our mouths.' In either case, men and women will have been freed forever from the burden and the splendour of the ruin at Babel. But which, one wonders, will be the greater silence?"*

UST AS MUCH as the word, silence is a creature of the alphabet: the pause between word and word, the silent contemplation of the text, the silence of meditative thought, are all forms of alphabetical silence. Even in our silence we are lettered men, at home on the island of history in the alphabetic domain. Most of us have, at best, only an inkling of the silence before words; and many of us have gone the opposite way, converting silence into something mechanical, into the no that separates beep from beep.

Genesis I:6–7 tells of the beginning of silence, silence before it became the stuff of history: When He hammered out the first gold foil (a word usually translated as the "firmament"), He separated the roaring waters below from the thundering waters above. With a three inch shard, or a glittering foil, silence began as an interstice, keeping the voices of Heaven and those of the Abyss apart. Silence was the first creature on the Earth. "Earth" grew from it. And that is the silence out of which, later, history took shape, as human voices made it vibrate.

This silence has vanished from the burnt-out world of Orwell's cipher. The "zero" that separates beeps has replaced it. And this one-zero-one, not silence, is the stuff from which the interface between Winston and Julia is made. After the self-betrayal of Room 101, these two post-humans are not only beyond words, they are also beyond "silence," and equally beyond the ability to refer to their co-presence with the personal pronoun "we." They have turned into an interactive assembly of two. The new Adam and Eve are the critters of a computer.

The conversation we had begun on the history of the spelled-out word ended for us as the search for the history of both "silence" and the "we." At each stage the "alphabetization of silence" precedes that of speech. Its genesis is the first character of the beta-bet, the Aleph.

The power of the silence that precedes utterance is described by an eighteenth-century rabbi, Mendel Torum of Rymanov, who asks what the Children of Israel could have actually heard, and what they in fact did hear, when they received the Ten Commandments. Some rabbis maintained that all the Commandments were spoken directly to the Children in the Divine Voice. Others said that the Israelites heard only the first two Commandments—"I am the Lord thy God" and "Thou shalt have no other Gods before me"—before being overwhelmed, no longer able to endure the Divine Voice, obliged to receive the remaining Commandments through Moses.

Mendel believed that not even the first two Commandments were delivered to the Children, but only silence. They heard only the *aleph*, the Hebrew character with which the first Commandment begins, the *aleph* of the word *ani* or *anokhi*: "I." Gershom Scholem comments on this theory: "The consonant *aleph* represents nothing more than the position taken by the larynx when a word begins with a vowel. Thus the *aleph* may be said to denote the source of all articulate sound." The *aleph*, then, the first character in the Hebrew phonetic system, itself stands for no sound, but instead commands the mouth to open, fixing the position of the lips for the next sound. The Kabbalists regard the *aleph* as the spiritual root of all the other characters, and out of that opening of the mouth, that utter silence, springs all human intercourse. Thus, as Scholem tells us, Rabbi Mendel transforms the revelation on Mount Sinai into an event pregnant with infinite meaning, but devoid of any specific meaning.

In Semitic script, silence cannot be recorded. No rabbi would ask his students to spell out a word; he wants them to know what the root looks like. Only the alphabet can conjure up silence and situate it on the page. First silence creeps between the letters and makes it feasible to spell instead of to read. Then Roman monks in charge of teaching Latin to the

A B C

Irish put interstices between words. Sentences are literally anatomized, disjointed into their individual words. Silence, recorded as an interval, does for language what the knife will do for the anatomist. It creates books made up of words rather than lines. Utterances, which the ear hears as a whole, are disarticulated into *lemas*, just as physicians in the late Middle Ages dismember bodies to make their organs visible. Like a knife, silence, when it is made visible, creates a text that is suited for the eye. And this is a precondition to grasp the text at one glance—to contemplate it in silence rather than to hear it at the rhythm of speech. Just as the "text" of the thirteenth century emerges from the visual perception of the order among parts of speech, some centuries later the modern organism will come into existence as the (conceptual) result of the physiological order between the path of a dissected organism.

Having pushed itself between parts of speech, silence now removes the ear from the page. It first created "words," now it creates a new kind of standoffish reader. This new reader looks at the page on the desk in the same attitude in which he looks at his own conscience during the confession that the Fourth Lateran Council exacts every year. The autobiographer engages in self-inquisition: He scrupulously tortures his conscience to give up its stubborn silence. Centuries later even the subconscious has to be brought to light on the couch. All by himself, this modern individual delves into a text written in the past by another, or sets out on the ever more lonely journey into the text that the past has left beneath the surface of his conscious self.

The alphabetization of silence has brought about the new

loneliness of the "I," and of an analytic *we. We* is now one line in a text brought into being by communication. Not the silence before words but the absence of messages in a chaos of noises precedes the establishment of an interactive pattern. The pretextual *we* of orality, the "ethnic" *we* that has been transcended through conscience, has disappeared from reality. We know that the history of silence is reflected in the transition from the ethnic to the analytic *we*.

The *we* that we have used emphatically in this book is morphologically an English plural. Semantically, however, it is close to a dual, for which English, some time during the Anglo-Saxon period, has lost a special form. Other Indo-Germanic languages—for instance, the Slavonic ones—have preserved this form. And, like thought and the word, like narration and the lie, *we* has a history.

The *we* on which we want to reflect is not the dual of these two authors, but the personal pronoun, with which he who speaks refers to the first person in the plural. Now, what is that first person? The answer is rather easy when we deal with person in the singular: "I," the first person, speaks to "you," the second person. In doing so, I tell you something about a third, who neither is speaking nor is being addressed. By addressing a person whom I designate "you," I make that person at that moment unique to me—and distinguish that "you" from any third: person or thing. Thus, *you* is almost as unique as *I*. Even abuse will not detract from the power intrinsic to the spoken *you* to establish this exquisite bond. Some people who have been tortured report that not pain, but the address of the policeman has broken them. In exact opposition to the tightly bound *you*, the third person has enormous scope. The third person includes whatever the first chooses to tell the second about. Every *you* contains the germ of a response—not so *her*, *him*, or *it*.

The first person usually does not call itself by its name. The first person uses a pro-noun, a word used instead of a name or noun. All languages have such a pronoun by which the speaker refers to himself, though the coloring implied—the gesture associated with the utterance—is different here and there. In Armenian or Iroquoian, the *I* is like an arrow by which the speaker points at him- or herself; in other languages, the *I* gives more the impression of a retreat, an act of assuming distance.

Etymologically, the *I* can be brazen, as it is in English, but it can just as well be hazy, as in Japanese, in which *I* is *watakusi domo*, which best translates: Yours Faithfully. But semantically both forms—the direct one and the euphemism—are equally clear self-references by the speaker. Proud or humble, aggressive or meek, depending on status, age, mood, or custom, the pronoun for the first person singular is unequivocal as no other term: It says, "He Who Speaks."

This univocal precision of the *I* is a condition for the formation of plurals. In fact, with almost the same directness with which all languages oppose the addressing *I* with a *you* who is addressed, they also provide some kind of *we*. Quite arguably, the opposition of *I* and *we* is a more fundamental category than the opposition of singular and plural. For the English speaker, it seems natural that the existence of a third person singular—the *he-she-it*—requires that there be a third person plural—a *they*. But this is just not so in all languages. The Turk feels nothing natural in learning the English plural. His noun designates a form of existence, primarily a quality and only then a thing that can be counted. The noun in Turkish turns into an object, in our sense, only when it is qualified by a term indicating enumeration. For the Turk the important difference lies between "dwelling space" and two, five, or even one "house." When he speaks to someone about something, he stresses the difference between essentials and that which can be numbered—not as we do: number one as opposed to any other number. Even in Turkish, however, the difference between the *I* and the *we* is clear. No language seems to lack a pronoun that says, "I and. . . ."

Yet, this "I and . . ." can contrast in many ways with the *I*. This is true even morphologically: The opposition of two different roots—"ego/no; I/we; ich/wir; ja/mi"—is by no means universal. On every continent there are languages in which the plural of *I* is *I*'s. From Southeast Asia to the Far East to Finland, to Alaska and to the Great Plains, there are people who have a morphological plural for the *I*, and often they use it next to another pronoun, derived from a different root. Languages with such a morphologically double *we* are very common, and frequently the two words are semantically distinct. There may be one pronoun that says, "I, you, and possibly others," and another that says, "I and others, but not you." A language as simple as Malay creates insuperable difficulties for some English speakers, because they cannot get used to this duplicity in the *we*. Kwakiutl seems to have still another *we*, one that excludes *you* because it stresses our tribe's cohesion—including its dead members.

The simplest way for the English speaker to get a sense of this semantic proliferation within the first person plural is to look at Neo-Melanesian, as Pidgin English is now proudly called. Pidgin is a "creole" language: its syntax has remained

A B C

Malayo-Polynesian but most of its words are English. Mi, that's me; you, that's you; yu-pela, that's you and your fellow; mi-pela, that's me and my fellow, my peer—me and those like me, in contrast with yu-pela, you and those like you. Yumi, that's you and me, used when the speaker includes you-others, but wants to stress his tie to you, to keep distance from the fellows. Otherwise, he could just say what comes easiest: yu-mipela, you people with me and my fellows, all together. But, of course, he could also just pick you, me, and one other, and say yu-mi-tripela, and exclude any others who happen to be within earshot.

Various languages even draw a time dimension into their we. Some Bantu tongues (the N'kosa for example) distinguish between the we that has already come into being, and the we that is hoped for. It can be argued that the Mongols and the Ewe in Dahomey can place the dimension of hope into the pronoun. They seem to have distinct ways of expressing we that depend on you having a chance to be our clansman, or being informed that we will not accept you as an in-law. The thou can thus become a budding we.

As we wrote this book we were aware of the semantic poverty of our pronoun. The modern we tells nothing about the intention of those who are the collective subject. Only in Spanish, men and women still remain distinct as nosotros y nosotras, but when men speak, they feel free to include women in nosotros. The modern we says nothing about our limits: If we are some, many, or innumerable. Our we reveals nothing to the person we address—if he is a part of us, expected to join us, recognized as a third person, seen as a stranger. And, finally, most importantly, our we is unable to state if each one

126

ought to be taken as the subject of the sentence; or if *we* are all of us together: *We* form a subject.

This plastic *we* does not tell you who we are. This is the *we* of propaganda, which can create any subject and demand that the person addressed identify with it; which says "you ought to be one of us"; and which is used by the missionary, the humanist, and the salesman. This impoverished, borderless *we* enables *us* to say that *we* (today) feel, think, and do certain things. A voracious *we*, it incorporates the speaker—even against his will. Publicity presupposes this kind of *we*. This *we* allows the user to dispense with us, to manage us. It is the *we* of the normal, of those who fit.

As the two of us wrote this book, the literary *we* constantly silenced us, a deafening silence that makes it impossible for the reader to know anything about the writer. Using this contemporary *we*, the speaker engages in semantic violence, incorporating groups, whose way of formulating the *we* is heterogeneous to that of the observer, and thus driving them into silence.

We are not fools enough to propose, even as a joke, to return to ethnic silence, the silent co-presence before words, language, and text came into being. We are children of the book. But in our sadness we are silly enough to long for the one silent space that remains open in our examined lives, and that is the silence of friendship.*

*For a definition of friendship, see the epigraph to this book.

Select Bibliography

". . . while utilizing and including these texts, I do not depart from the conviction that a work of synthesis must rest mainly upon facts already gathered and critically digested by the relevant specialists: In other words upon what, from the standpoint of scholarship, must be classed as secondary sources. Those who are suspicious of this foundation show a distaste for the function of interpretation rather than a rationally grounded distrust of the method. All general views are, of course, open to correction, both as to fact and as to interpretation. . . ."

Lewis Mumford, *The Culture of Cities*

This bibliography contains mainly two types of books: the kind that will enable the reader to deepen and widen his knowledge of the subject, and those which, though not covering specifically the field of the present volume, have been drawn upon for special documentation.

Abernethy, Seonaid. "The Decisions Themselves: China, Vernacular Procedures; Japan, Vernacular Agreements." Unpublished typescript, 1985.

Adamson, J. W. "The Extent of Literacy in England in the Fifteenth and Sixteenth Centuries." *The Library* 10, no. 2 (September 1929): 163.

In 1489, the rule concerning the "benefit of the clergy" was changed; it was a privilege that laymen who could read had enjoyed with the clergy. By 1489, so many laymen had become literate that a distinction was drawn between them and the ordained clergy.

Altaner, Berthold. "Die Heransbildung eines einheimischen Klerus in der Mission des 13. and 14. Jahrhunderts." *Zeitschrift für Missionswissenshaft* 18 (1928): 193-208.

_____. "Sprachstudien und Sprachkenntnisse im Dienste der Mission des 13. und 14. Jahrhunderts." *Zeitschrift für Missionswissenschaft* 21 (1931): 113-36.

_____. "Die fremdsprachliche Ausbildung der Dominikanermissionare während des 13. und 14. Jahrhunderts." *Zeitschrift für Missionswissenschaft* 23 (1933): 233-71.

_____. "Raymundus Lullus und der Sprachenkanon (can. 11) des Konzils von Vienne (1312)." *Historisches Jahrbuch* 53 (1933): 190-219.

_____. "Zur Kenntnis des Arabischen im 13. und 14. Jahrhunderts." *Orientalia Christiana Periodica* (Rome) 2 (1936): 437-52. See Steiner.

Amelotti, M., and G. Costamagna. "Alle origini del notariato italiano." *Studi storici sul notariato italiano* 2 (Rome) (1975). See Clanchy.

Asensio, Eugenio. "La lengua compañera del imperio: História de una idea de Nebrija en España y Portugal." *Revista de Filologia Española* 43 (1960): 399-413. See Heisig.

Auerbach, Erich. "Dante's Address to the Reader." *Romance Philology* 7 (1954): 268-78.

_____. *Literatursprache und Publikum in der lateinischen Spätantike und im Mittelalter*. Bern: 1958.

Bahner, Werner. "Beitrag zum Sprachbewusstsein in der spanischen Literature des 16. und 17. Jahrhunderts." *Neue Beiträge zur Literaturwissenschaft*. Berlin: Rüttner, 1956. See Heisig.

Balogh, Joseph. "Voces paginorum." *Philologus* 82 (1926/27): 84-109 and 202-40. See Saenger.

Battisti, Carlo. "Secoli Illetterati. Appunti sulla crisi del Latino prima della riforma carolingia." *Studi Medievali* (1960): 369-96.

A B C

Bauml, Franz. "Der Uebergang muendlicher zur artes-bestimmten Literatur des Mittelalters. Gedanken und Bedenken." *Fachliteratur des Mittelalters: Festschrift für Gerhard Eis*, 1-10. Stuttgart: Metzler, 1968.

———. "Varieties and Consequences of Medieval Literacy and Illiteracy." *Speculum* 55, no. 2 (1980): 237-65.

Bauml, Franz, and Edda Spielmann. "From Illiteracy to Literacy: Prologomena to a Study of the Nibelungenlied." In Duggan, *Oral Literature*, 62-73.

Bayer, Hans. "Zur Soziologie des mittelalterlichen Individualisierungsprosesses: Ein Beitrag zu einer wirklichkeitsbezogenen Geistesgeschichte." *Archiv fuer Kulturgeschichte* 58 (1976): 115-53.

See Morris.

Beardsley, Monroe C. "Aspects of Orality: A Short Commentary." *New Literary History* 8, no. 3 (1977): 521-34.

Belting, Hans. *Das Bild und sein Publikum im Mittelalter Form und Funktion früher Bildtafeln der Passion Gebr.* Reihe: Mann Studio, 1981.

See Daly.

Benson, Larry D. "The Literary Character of Anglo-Saxon Formulaic Poetry." *Publication of the Modern Language Association* 81 (1966): 334-41.

Berman, Harold J. "The Background of the Western Legal Tradition in the Folklaw of the Peoples of Europe." *University of Chicago Law Review* 45, no. 3 (Spring 1978): 553-97.

Deals with the *disembedding* of the law, through codification, since the late eleventh century: "There was a time, prior to the late eleventh century when the peoples of Western Europe were not conscious of any clear distinction between legal institutions and other institutions of social coherence. . ."

See Watkins.

Berthold, Luise. "Mittelalterliche Sprachwörter und das moderne Mundartwörterbuch." *Hessische Blätter für Volkskunde* 39 (1940): 64-67.

Many proverbs for which we have evidence from medieval

130

sources are carried almost unchanged into contemporary dialects as dialectological dictionaries will show.
See Ohly.

Best, Edward E. "Attitudes Toward Literacy Reflected in Petronius." *Transactions of the American Philosophical Association* 81 (1955): 112-39.
Tries to take an intermediary position between Frederick G. Kenyon, *Books and Readers in Ancient Greece and Rome* (Oxford: Clarendon Press, 1951, 2d ed.), who believed that few people read to themselves, and Helen Tanzer, *The Common People of Pompeii: A Study of the Graffiti* (Baltimore: Johns Hopkins University Press, 1939), who after examining 15,000 such graffiti came to believe that almost everyone could read and write.
See Riché.

Betz, Werner. *Deutsch und lateinische: Die Lehnbildungen der althochdeutschen Benediktinerregel.* Bonn: Bouvier, 1965.
Examines the ninth-century translation of St. Benedict's Rule into Old German, focusing attention on the German expressions that had to be coined or reinterpreted in the process. With much more detail, Ibach and Schwarz follow the same events in the formation of Frankish.

Bien, G. "Lüge." *Historisches Wörterbuch der Philosophie.* Eds. Joachim Ritter and K. Grunder. Vol. 5. Basel: Schwabe, 1980.
See Furhmann.

Bischoff, Bernard. *Die südostdeutschen Schreibschulen and Bibliotheken in der Karolingerzeit.* Vols. 1 and 2. Leipzig: O. Harrassowitz, 1940.
See Riché.

————. "The Study of Foreign Languages in the Middle Ages." *Speculum* 36, no. 2 (April 1961): 209-24.
See Steiner.

————. "Elementarunterricht und probationes pennae in der ersten Hälfte des Mittelalters." *Mittelalteriche Studien* 1 (1966): 74-87.
See Riché.

————. *Paläographie des römischen Altertums und des abendlän-*

dischen Mittelalters. Grundlagen der Germanistik 24. Berlin: Eric Schmidt, 1979.

See Wattenbach.

Bischoff, Bernard, and Joseph Hoffman. *Libri Sancti Kyliani: die Würzburger Schreibschule und die Dombibliothek im 8. und 9. Jahrhunderts.* Würzburg: Schonigh, 1952.

See Riché.

Blidstein, Gerald. "Maimonides on 'Oral Law.'" *The Jewish Law Annual* 1 (1978): 108-22.

See Watkins.

Bloch, R. Howard. *Etymologies and Genealogies: A Literary Anthropology of the French Middle Ages.* Chicago: University of Chicago Press, 1983.

Bonaventure, Brother. "The Teaching of Latin in Later Medieval England." *Mediaeval Studies* 23 (1961): 1-20.

See Riché.

Borst, Arno. *Der Turmbau von Babel: Geschichte der Meinungen über Ursprung und Vielfalt der Sprachen und Völker.* 4 vols. Stuttgart: Hierseman, 1957-63.

The commentary on the Genesis story about the Tower of Babel has given rise to a vast and rich outpouring of opinion about language. In an encyclopedic fashion, the author gathers and orders the issues discussed: Is language a gift from God or a creation of man? Did Adam speak Hebrew or some tongue like German? What relationship is there between a people and a tongue? What does the multiplicity of tongues "mean"? A complementary question is treated by Pinborg: the thirteenth-century philosophical theories about the "modes of meaning."

Bossong, Georg. *Probleme der Übersetzung wissenschaftlicher Werke aus dem Arabischen in das Altspanische zur Zeit Alfons des Weisen.* Tübingen: Max Niemeyer, 1979.

See Steiner.

Bowra, C. M. *Heroic Poetry.* London: Macmillan, 1951.

_____. *In General and Particular.* Clayton Memorial Lecture Delivered Before the Manchester Literary and Philosophical Society. Cleveland and New York: The World Publishing Company, 1959.

Boyd, Beverly. *Chaucer and the Medieval Book*. San Marino: The Huntington Library Publications, 1973.

Brach, Carla Casetti. "Donne copiste nella leggenda di Bisanzio." *Orientalia Christiana Periodica* 39 (1973): 478-89.
See Grundmann.

Braybrooke, E. K. "Custom as a Source of English Law." *Michigan Law Review* 50, no. 1 (1951): 71-94.
See Watkins.

Bresslau, Harry. *Handbuch der Urkundlenlehre für Deutschland und Italien*. 2 vols. Leipzig: Veit and Company, 1912.
Remains the fundamental handbook for all studies of medieval literacy.
See Wattenbach.

Brincken, Anna Dorothee von den. "Zur Universalkarthographie des Mittelalters." *Miscellanea Mediaevalia* 7 (1970): 249-78.
See Daly.

_____. "Tabula alphabetica: von den Anfängen alphabetische Registerarbeiten zu Geschichtswerken." In *Festschrift für Hermann Heimpel*. Max Planck Institut für Geschichte. Göttingen: Vandenhoeck & Ruprecht, 1972.
See Daly.

Bynum, David E. "The Generic Nature of Oral Epic Poetry." *Genre* Five, 2, no. 3 (September 1969): 236-58.
For Homer and much of pre-Platonic Greece *aoide* means both the art of epic singing and the song itself. Where the song does not survive the singing, no distinction between the two can be made. And *epos* means "words" or "utterances." Using the term in this sense, the "epic" and the "oral" tradition coincide. Parry's criteria to recognize the epic nature of a text directly apply only to one small segment of the world's epic treasures: those which, like Homer, can be classified with Aristotle as having a simple meter and unlimited narration. Bynum argues that the epic tradition is much wider than that, has been accumulated by

different hands, for over 150 years, by different methods, belongs to different genres, with some appearing here, others only there. No one specialist can know more than one of the other languages in which it has been noted down.

_____. *The Daemon in the Wood: A Study of Oral Narrative Patterns*. Cambridge: Harvard University Press, 1978. Published by the Center for the Study of Oral Literature.

This study represents a search for the kind of ideas that find their expression in oral tradition, and the web of their concatenations. It is interested in the narrative per se, and not as a vehicle reflecting social structure, manifesting dynamics of character, reinforcing custom or law. Discovers "a protean ability of one finite complex of oral traditional fictions to conform with any mode of action or being that men have adopted." Bynum searches for these ideas also in puzzles, sayings, and tales.

Carpenter, Rhys. "The Antiquity of the Greek Alphabet." *American Journal of Anthropology* 37 (1933):8-29.

Certeau, Michel de, Dominique Julia, and Jacques Revel. *Une Politique de la langue: la Révolution française et les patois: L'enquête de Grégoire*. Paris: Gallimard, 1975.

Between 1792 and 1794, the unification of the French language had top priority within the Revolution. Abbé Grégoire was charged with a national survey of vernaculars, and the attitudes toward them are analyzed by the authors: "La langue française et plus faite pour prier le Créateur suprême et chanter ses langages." The French language is much better suited than the dialects to sing the praises of the supreme creator . . . it is necessary to sacrifice these on the altar of the Revolution . . . one can feel that the "patois" is too heavy, too rough and too dull: not quite worthy of God. The patois encourages laziness, superstition, and inquisition. Its destruction can only be agreeable to God and politics will not lose anything by it.
See Heisig.

Chaytor, H. J. "The Medieval Reader and Textual Criticism." *Bulletin of the John* (Rylands University Library) 26 (1941): 49-56. See Saenger.

_____. *From Script to Print: An Introduction to Medieval Vernacular Literature*. Cambridge: Cambridge University Press, 1945.

Pages 5-21 develop his previously stated idea that the invention of printing was the main factor leading from loud to silent reading.

See Saenger.

Cheney, Christopher Robert. *Notaries Public in England in the Thirteenth and Fourteenth Centuries*. Oxford: Clarendon Press, 1972.

See Clanchy.

Chenu, Marie Dominique. *L'éveil de la conscience dans la civilisation médiévale*. Conference Albert-Le-Grand 1968. Montreal: Institut d'études médiévales, 1969.

See Clanchy.

Christin, Anne-Marie, ed. *Ecriture: systèmes idéographiques et pratique expressive*. Paris: Le Sycamore, 1982.

Clanchy, M. T. "Remembering the Past and the Good Old Law." *History* 40 (1970): 165-76.

_____. *From Memory to Written Record: England 1066–1307*. Cambridge: Harvard University Press, 1979.

Reviews what we know of growing literacy in the West during a 250-year period from a new point of view, stressing not what it contributed to literature and "science," but the way it changed (or reflected a change) in self-perception and the perception of society. The conversation that started *ABC* grew out of our attempt to bring insights, acquired from the school of Milman Parry, into the questions asked by Clanchy. For the history of the notaries who did much of the writing, see Cheney and Amelotti. Sheehan focuses on just one of their major tasks: the alphabetization of the last will. Franklin observes a rapid increase of lay literacy between 1050 and 1200 in Russia, even though charters have much less importance there than in the West. Vollrath looks at the vernacular records of Anglo-Saxon laws. She believes that effective legislation was to a large extent independent from the written record, which was often made much later. She points to the difficulties of reconstructing from Latin records the Germanic expression behind the Latin formula that is preserved. In Paravicini, volume 5, pages 71-116 deal with the impact of increasing literary activity on the style of administration in the Middle Ages.

Classen, Peter, ed. *Recht und Schrift im Mittelalter*. Vorträge und Forschungen 23. Sigmaringen: Thorbecke, 1977.

See Watkins.

Constable, Giles. *The Letters of Peter the Venerable*. Cambridge: Harvard University Press, 1967.

Contamine, Philippe. "L'écrit et l'oral en France à la fin du Moyen Age." In Paravicini, pp. 102-115.

See Clanchy.

Cormier, Raymond J. "The Problem of Anachronism: Recent Scholarship on the French Medieval Romances of Antiquity." *Philological Quarterly* 53 (1974): 145-57.

Cox, James M. "Autobiography and America." *The Virginia Quarterly Review* 47, no. 2 (Spring 1971): 252-77.

Cressy, David, *Literacy and the Social Order: Reading and Writing in Tudor and Stuart England*. Cambridge: Cambridge University Press, 1980.

Crosby, Ruth. "Oral Delivery in the Middle Ages." *Speculum* 11, no. 1 (January 1936): 88-110.

Points out that the direct address to the *reader* as opposed to the *listener* first becomes popular in literature in the fifteenth century; with Lydgate's Troy Book.

_____. "Chaucer and the Custom of Oral Delivery." *Speculum* 13, no. 4 (October 1938): 413-32.

Culley, Robert C. *Oral-Formulaic Language in the Biblical Psalms*. Toronto: Toronto University Press, 1967.

Curshmann, Michael. "Oral Poetry in Medieval English, French, and German Literature: Some Notes on Recent Research." *Speculum* 42 (1967): 36-52.

_____. "The Concept of Oral Formula as Impediment to Our Understanding of Medieval Oral Poetry." *Medievalia et Humanistica*. New Series 8: 63-76.

Curtius, Ernst Robert. *European Literature and the Latin Middle Ages*. Princeton: Princeton University Press, 1973.

He covers the book, page, and letters as symbols in Western

culture up to the thirteenth century. Much more detail and quotations can be found in Koep, Rauch, and Rothacker. Nobis presents a short survey. Weinerich analyzes the metaphors used for "remembrance," and finds two ideal types: the storage room and the wax tablet.

Meier examines the symbols used by Hildegard von Bingen to speak of "forgetting"; mainly man forgetting God and God forgetting man.

However, Meier's article is the best critical guide to research on such symbols in the Middle Ages for remembrance and forgetting in general. Harms focuses only on nature insofar as it "speaks," mainly through the voice of God's writing that speaks to illiterate and literate alike. Nobis addresses the contrast between de-ciphering the Creator's handwriting in nature and the description of nature that constitutes modern science and turns the "book" topsy-turvy. Krafft, Schilling, and Ohly pursue the literary use of the book as symbol and as emblematic element during the following centuries. The use of the book as a symbol for spiritual reality can be found in Leclercq and Kretzenbacher. That God has revealed himself not only through letters but also through ruler and circle is a point made by Ohly (*Deus Geometra*). Meier ("Verhaeltnis") studies the relationship between the text of Hildegard and the miniatures by which it is illustrated.

Daly, L. W., and B. A. Daly. "Some Techniques in Mediaeval Latin Lexicography." *Speculum* 39 (1964): 231-39.

Isidore of Seville in his *Etymologiae* had already tried an alphabetic arrangement by first and second letters. But only in 1053 did Papias begin to arrange entries in his dictionary in a fully alphabetic order; for quotations he used abbreviations indicated in a table at the beginning of his work. Brincken deals with the first alphabetic indices starting in the early thirteenth century. Rouse, pp. 29-40, provides a full introduction to the history of the chapter and the verse in the Bible, and reference methods in the late Middle Ages; his work is complemented by Halporn. Rouse ("Early Library") reports on the origins of random access to library books, and Goetz on the appearance of encyclopedias. The world map might be considered as a particular form of ran-

dom access description (see Brincken). On library buildings, see
Knowles. For the contents of a private library (1271), belonging
to Gérard d'Abéville, the adversary of Thomas Aquinas, see
Grabmann, pp. 16ff.

D'Angelo, Frank J. "Luria and Literacy: The Cognitive Consequences of Reading and Writing." In *Literacy as a Human Problem*, ed. James C. Raymond.

David, M. "Le serment du sacre du IXe au XVe siècle. Contribution à l'étude des limites juridiques de la souveraineté." *Revue
du moyen âge Latin* 6 (1950): 5-272.

Davison, J. A. "Literature and Literacy in Ancient Greece." *Phoe-
nix* 16 (1962): 141-56 and 219-33.

De Ghellinck, S. *L'essort de la litterature latine au 12. siècle.* Brussels:
Desclée de Brouwer, 1954.
See Leclercq.

Diamond, Stanley. "The Rule of Law Versus the Order of Custom."
In *The Rule of Law*, ed. R. P. Wolf. New York: Simon and Schus-
ter, 1971.
This article comments on the distinction made by Paul Gohan-
nan that law has no essence, but only a definable historical nature. Compare this with the comment of Paul Radin: "A custom
is in no sense a part of our properly functioning culture. It belongs definitely to the past. At best it is moribund."
See Watkins.

Diringer, David. *The Alphabet: A Key to the History of Mankind.* 2d
ed., rev. New York: Philosophical Library, 1953.

Duby, Georges. "Structures de parente et noblesse dans la France
du Nord au XIe et XIIe siècles." In *Hommes et structures du
Moyen Âge*, ed. Georges Duby. Paris: Mouton, 1973.
See pp. 282-83 for notion of restructuring and reordering of
aristocratic lineage from horizontal to vertical due to influence
of the *text*.

Duggan, Joseph, ed. *Oral Literature. Seven Essays.* Edinburgh and
London: Scottish Academic Press, 1975.

Duggan, Joseph J. *The Song of Roland: Formulaic Style and Poetic
Craft.* Berkeley: University of California Press, 1973.

Eickelman, Dale E. "The Art of Memory: Islamic Education and its Social Reproduction." *Comparative Studies in Society and History* 20 (1978): 485-516.

Eisenstein, Elisabeth. *The Printing Press as an Agent of Change: Communications and Cultural Transformations in Early-Modern Europe.* 2 vols. Cambridge: Cambridge University Press, 1979.

The author was upset by the oracular style with which McLuhan raised an obviously important and so far little understood event: the effect of printing on written records, and on the views of elites. Her theme is not the shift from an oral to a literate culture, but the shift from one kind of literate culture to another during the fifteenth century: the move from "scribal" or "chirographic" to print or typographic culture.

On the way in which scribal procedures and the changing appearance of the handwritten page affected twelfth-to-fourteenth-century literature, see Chaytor. The most brilliantly illustrated history showing the development of writing styles, binding, illustrations, and reference methods, the changing role of the unprinted book in the monastery, university, and in general culture, its relation to lay piety and enjoyment and self-perception are the pages devoted to the manuscript in Martin.

See also Steinberg.

Ernout, A. "Dictáre, 'dicter,' allem. dichten." *Revue des Etudes Latines* 29 (1951): 155-61.

Ewert, A. "Dante's Theory of Language." *Modern Language Review* 35 (1940): 355-65.

Febvre, Lucien, and Henry-Jean Martin. *L'Apparition du Livre.* Paris: Editions Albin Michel, 1958.

Feigl, Helmuth. "Von der mundlichen Rechtsweisung zur Aufzeichnung. Die Entstehung der Weistumer und verwandter Quellen." In Classen, *Recht und Schrift.*

See Watkins.

Felder, Hilarin. *Geschichte der wissenschaftlichen Studien im Franziskanerorden bis um die Mitte des 13. Jahrhunderts.* Freiburg im Breisgau: Herder, 1904.

See Steiner.

Finnegan, Ruth, ed. *A World Treasury of Oral Poetry.* Bloomington: Indiana University Press, 1978.

A B C

Foley, John Miles. "The Traditional Oral Audience." *Balkan Studies* 18 (1977): 145-53.

―――――. "Oral Literature: Premises and Problems." *Choice* 18 (1980): 487-96.

This article is written primarily with the acquisition librarian of a college library in mind, and includes a list of easily available sound recordings of oral texts. For orientation on the ramifications of studies generated by Parry's history of controversies and progress. For partly unpublished research on oral traditions around the globe, see Lord ("Perspectives"). The footnotes in Peabody are an excellent introduction to the state of knowledge.

Fraenger, Wilhelm. *Der Bauernbruegel and das deutsche Sprichwort.* Munich and Leipzig: E. Rentsch, 1923.

Analyzes a painting in which Peter Brueghel the Elder in 1559 has preserved a dozen sayings about the world upside down. See Ohly.

Franklin, Simon. "Literacy and Documentation in Early Medieval Russia." *Speculum* 60, no. 1 (1985): 1-38.
See Clanchy.

Fry, Donald K. "Themes and Type-Scenes in Elene: 1-113." *Speculum* 44 (1969): 34-45.

Hypothesizes a survival of formulaic techniques in written poetry from an earlier tradition.

Frye, Northrop. *The Great Code: The Bible and Literature.* New York and London: Harcourt Brace Jovanovich, 1982.

Fuhrmann, Horst. "Die Fälschungen im Mittelalter: Überlegungen zum mittelalterlichen Wahrheitsbegriff." *Historische Zeitschrift* 197 (1963): 529-34.

Forgeries abound during the Middle Ages—not only forgeries of charters, but those of relics and of "authorships." Many works are ascribed to Augustine, Ambrose, and Cicero that they could not have written. This raises two questions: What is the motive for these forgeries, and why were they accepted? The author sees this mainly as a result of the medieval desire to correct the "order of things" to fit the forger's opinion of how the order should be. The increase of documents during the twelfth century lends itself particularly to this corrective enterprise. For a short introduction to the history of *falsiloquium* and *mendacium* see Bien; and for more extensive historical documentation see Müller. About Herodotus on lying, see Hartog.

Galbraith, Vivian Hunter. "The Literacy of the Medieval English Kings." Raleigh Lecture on History 10 July 1935. In *Proceedings of the British Academy*, XXI (1935): 201-38.

Gannim, John M. *Style and Consciousness in Middle English Narrative*. Princeton: Princeton University Press, 1983.

Ganshof, François L. "Charlemagne et l'usage de l'écrit en matière administrative." *Le Moyen Age* 57 (1951): 1-25.
See Clanchy.

Gellrich, Jesse M. *The Idea of the Book in the Middle Ages: Language Theory, Mythology, and Fiction*. Ithaca: Cornell University Press, 1985.

Giesecke, Michael. " 'Volkssprache' und 'Verschriftlichung des Lebens' im Spätmittelalter—am Beispiel der Genese der gedrukten Frachprosa in Deutschland." In Gumbrecht, *Literatur*, 39-67.

Gilson, Etienne. *Heloise and Abelard*. Ann Arbor: University of Michigan Press, 1960.

Glauche, Gunther. "Schullektüren im Mittelalter. Entstehung und Wandlung des Lektürenkanons bis 1200 an Quellen dargestellt." *Muenchner Beiträge zur Medievistik und Renaissanceforschung* 5. Munich, 1970.
See Riché.

Goetz, Walter. "Die Enzyklopädien des 13. Jahrhundert: Ein Beitrag zur Entstehung der Laienbildung." *Zeitschrift fuer deutsche Geistesgeschichte* 2, no. 6 (1936): 227-50.
See Daly.

Goody, Jack. "The Consequences of Literacy." In Jack Goody, ed. *Literacy in Traditional Societies*. Cambridge: Cambridge University Press, 1968.

————. *The Domestication of the Savage Mind*. Cambridge: Cambridge University Press, 1977.

————, ed. *Literacy in Traditional Societies*. Cambridge: Cambridge University Press, 1968.

Grabmann, Martin. *Mittelalterliches Geistesleben*. Munich: Huebner, 1926.

Reconstructs the library of an adversary of Thomas A. Gerard d'Abéville, who donated his library in 1271. A catalogue was made in 1338.

See Daly.

Graff, Harvey J. *The Literacy Myth: Literacy and Social Structure in the Nineteenth Century*. New York, San Francisco, and London: Academic Press, 1979.

————, ed. *Literacy and Social Development in the West*. Cambridge Studies in Oral and Literate Culture. Cambridge: Cambridge University Press, 1981.

Greenfield, Kathleen. "Changing Emphasis in English Vernacular Homiletic Literature." *Journal of Medieval History* 7, no. 3 (1981): 283-97.

Grundmann, Herbert. "Die Frauen und die Literatur im Mittelalter. Ein Beitrag zur Frage nach der Entstehung des Schrifttums in der Volkssprache." *Archiv fuer Kulturgeschichte* 26 (1935): 129-61.

————. "Litteratus—illiteratus. Der Wandel einer Bildungsnorm vom Altertum zum Mittelalter." *Archiv fuer Kulturgeschichte* 40 (1958): 1-65.

————. *Religiöse Bewegungen im Mittelalter. Untersuchungen über die geschichtlichen Zusammenhänge zwischen der Ketzerei, den Bettelorden und der religiösen Frauenbewegung im 12. und 13. Jahrhunderts und über die geschichtlichen Grundlagen der Deutschen Mystik*. Darmstadt: Wissenschaftel Buchges, 1970.

The spread of literacy in the twelfth century cannot be separated from the religious movements, especially among the laity. Grundmann strongly reacts against interpretations that explain these movements stressing predominantly social and economic causes; for him Church-bound and heretic movements are ultimately motivated by the desire to effect religious reform based on the reading of scriptures. In the course of this movement, the relationship between clerical status and literacy changed in a complex fashion.

See Grundmann (*Litteratus*) and Thompson on the possibility of combining lay-status with emerging literacy, versus Clanchy, part II, 7 and Gilson's discussion of Abelard's status. *I Laici* contains several papers referring to this point; see in particular, Huyghebaert on the status of women, and Grundmann (*Frauen*) on the contribution of women toward literacy in the vernacular tongues. Also, in Eastern Europe, Franklin notices the increase in lay literacy, and Brach notices the increase of women scribes—at least in the legends of Byzantium.

Gumbrecht, Hans Ulrich. *Literatur in der Gesellschaft des Spätmittelalters*. (Grundriss der romanischen Literaturen des Mittelalters), Vol. 1. Heidelberg: Carl Winter, 1980.
See Clanchy.

Hajdu, Helga. *Das Mnemotechnische Schrifttum des Mittelalters*. Amsterdam: E. J. Bonset, 1967.

Hajnal, István. *L'Enseignement de l'écriture aux universités médiévales*. Budapest: Academia Scientiarum Hungarica Budapestini, 1954.

Halporn, J. W. "Methods of Reference in Cassiodorus." *Journal of Library History* 16 (1981): 71-91.

Hanning, R. W. *The Individual in the Twelfth-Century Romances*. New Haven: Yale University Press, 1977.

Harms, Wolfgang, and Heimo Reinitzer. *Natura Loquax: Naturkunde und allegorische Naturdeutung vom Mittelalter bis zur fruehen Neuzeit*. Mikrokosmos: Beitraege zur Literatur-wissenschaft und Bedeutungsforschung Bd. 7. Frankfort: Lang, 1981.
Nature speaks; in fact, Nature might be chatty. But how to learn Nature's language? And who are those who can understand its language and make it understandable?
See Curtius.

Hartog, François. *Le miroir d'Hérodote: Essai sur la représentation de l'autre*. Paris: Gallimard, 1980.
Cicero (*Laws* I, 1, 5) calls Herodotus both the Father of History,

and a Liar: "Quamquam et apud Herodtum, patrem Historiae
. . . sunt innumerabilis fabulae. . . ." Hartog retraces the his-
tographic stages in which "Herodotus' lies" were differently
understood: as a propagandist, a plagiarist, and only slowly as a
maturing author, as he has been known for three successive generations since the mid-nineteenth century.

Veyne, however, might be more correct: the father of history was
in no way bound by history's supposed rules. Herodotus still
knows equally well what he has seen, been told of, or has understood. Somewhat like Plato, he sits on the watershed at which
our kind of "lie" starts as a tiny brook.

Harvey, David. "Greeks and Romans Learn to Write." In Havelock
and Hershbell, *Communication Arts*, 63-80.
See Riché.

Harvey, F. D. "Literacy in the Athenian Democracy." *Revue des
Études Grecques* 79 (1966): 585-635.
See Riché.

Harvey, L. P. "Oral Composition and the Performance of Novels
of Chivalry in Spain." In Duggan, *Oral Literature*, 84-100.

Hatcher, Elisabeth R. "The Moon and Parchment: Paradiso II,
73-78." *Dante Studies* 89 (1971): 55-60.

Havelock, Eric. *Preface to Plato*. Cambridge: Harvard University
Press, 1963.

Suggests that even after the waning of the epic tradition, and the
rise of specific literary forms of poetry, oral culture substantially
prevailed until Plato, whose "war against the poets" in *The Re-
public* is to be explained as an attack on the bases of the older
civilization of the spoken word by the greatest representative of
the new age of prose, science, abstract thought, and writing.
Havelock goes far beyond Parry, who could not have admitted
that an "oral culture" could exist without the living tradition of
oral poetry which determines its character.

————. "Prologue to Greek Literacy." In *Lectures in Memory of
Louise Taft Sample. University of Cincinnati Classical Studies*, vol.

2. Norman, Oklahoma: University of Oklahoma Press, 1973: 331-91.

_____. "The Preliteracy of the Greeks." *New Literary History* 8, no. 3 (1977): 369-91.

_____. "The Ancient Art of Oral Poetry." *Philosophy and Rhetoric* 12, no. 3 (Summer 1979): 187-202.

_____. *The Literate Revolution in Greece and Its Cultural Consequences*. Princeton: Princeton University Press, 1982.

Havelock, Eric A., and Jackson P. Hershbell, eds. *Communication Arts in the Ancient World*. Humanistic Studies in the Communication Arts. New York: Hastings House, 1978.

Haymes, Edward R. *A Bibliography of Studies Relating to Parry's and Lord's Oral Theory*. Publications of the Milman Parry Collection. Cambridge: Harvard University Press, 1973.
See Foley.

Heck, Philipp. *Uebersetzungsprobleme im fruehen Mittelalter*. Tübingen: Mohr, 1931.
Analyzes early medieval Latin texts in which Germanic vernacular custom or law has been codified. Searches for the vernacular expressions that may have given rise to the use of the Latin formulas, an activity in which Heck has to engage in order to interpret the text. Insists, however, on sticking to the Latin terminology when translating this text into German, fully aware that some other Germanic expression than the one he has guessed at might have been lying behind the Latin term.

Hedwig, Klaus. *Sphaera Lucis. Studien zur Intelligibilität des seienden im Kontext der mittelalterlichen Lichtspekulation*. Beiträge zur Geschichte der Philosophie und Theologie des Mittelalters NF Bd. 18. Munster: Aschendorf, 1980.
See Curtius.

Heer, Friedrich. *The Medieval World: Europe 1100-1500*. New York and Toronto: New American Library, 1961.
See Morris.

Heisig, Karl. "Muttersprache: ein romanistischer Beitrag zur

Genesis eines deutschen Wortes und zur Entstehung der deutsch-franzoesischen Sprachgrenze." *Muttersprache* 22, no. 3 (1954): 144-74.

The connection between "mother" and "tongue" is first made in Lorraine in the tenth century, at the time of a retreat of the Frankish and the advance of neo-Latin speaking populations. Monks of the reform abbey of Gorz used it in opposition to *patrius sermo*. *Lingua materna* appealed to the women to maintain their speechform. It appears in Latin sermon notes meant to be delivered in vernacular tongues. During the twelfth to fourteenth centuries, the term—if used—was opposed to Latin, used to designate a lower type of language. In the fourteenth century, it was used only in the business language of the Hansa. Asensio examines Nebrija's idea of the national language being a camp follower. Weissberger retraces the rise of the idea of "mother tongue" in European cultures. Josten and Bahner give easy access to source material on the subject. We know of not one attempt to retrace the history of the corresponding idea: that *homo* is naturally *monolinguis*.

Hilty, G. "Die Romanisierungen in den Strassburger Eiden." *Vox Romanica* 25 (1966): 227-35.

See Schmidt-Wiegand.

Hoekstra, A. *Homeric Modifications of Formulaic Prototypes. Studies in the Development of Greek Epic Diction.* Amsterdam: North-Holland Publishing Co., 1965.

Holoka, James P. "Homeric Originality: A Survey." *Classical World* 66, no. 5 (1973): 257-93.

See Foley.

Horner, Winifred Bryan, ed. *The Present State of Scholarship in Historical and Contemporary Rhetoric.* Columbia and London: University of Missouri Press, 1983.

See Chapter 2, "The Middle Ages," by James J. Murphy.

Howard, Donald R. "The Canterbury Tales: Memory and Form." *English Language History* 38 (1971): 319-28.

————. *The Idea of the Canterbury Tales.* Berkeley and Los Angeles: University of California Press, 1976.

Huyghebaert, Nicolas. "Les femmes laïques dans la vie religieuse des 11e et 12e siècles dans la province Ecclésiastique de Reims." In *I Laici nella Societas Christiana*, 345-95.
See Grundmann.

Ibach, Helmut. "Zu Wortschatz und Begriftswelt der althochdeutschen Benediktinerregel." *Beiträge zur Geschichte der deutschen Sprache und Literatur* (Halle). 78 (1956): 1-110; 79 (1957): 106-85; 80 (1958): 190-271; 81 (1959): 123-73; 82 (1960): 371-74f.
See Betz.

I Laici nella Societas Christiana. De sec. 11 and 12. Atti della terza Settimana internazionale di studio, Mendola agosto 1965. Publicazioni dell Universitá Cattolica del Sacro uore, ser. III, varia 5. Milan, 1966.
See Grundmann.

Inter Documentation Publishing Company. *Emblem Books*. 354 Titles on microfiche. Zurich, 1983.
See Ohly.

Jaeger, Werner. *Platos Stellung Aufbau der griechischen Bildung*. Berlin, 1928.
See Riché.

Jarecki, Walter. *Signa Loquendi. Die cluniscensischen Signa-Listen eingeleitet und herausgegeben*. Saecula Spiritalia Bd. 4. Baden-Baden: Korner, 1981.
Monastic sign language of the High Middle Ages.

Jeggrey, David. *By Things Seen: Reference and Recognition in Medieval Thought*. Ottawa: University of Ottawa Press, 1979.
See Daly.

Josten, Dirk. *Sprachvorbild und Sprachnorm im Urteil des 16. und 17. Jahrhunderts. Sprachlandschertliche Prioritäten, Sprachautoritäten, Sprachimmanente Argumentation*. Europ. Hochschulschriften R 1, 152. Bern: Frankfurt, 1976.
Critical and annotated collection of opinions expressed by German poets and savants—see Heisig.

Jousse, Marcel. *Le Style oral rhythmique et mnémotechnique chez les Verbomoteurs*. Paris: G. Beauchesne, 1925.

A B C

Kailaspathy, K. *Tamil Heroic Poetry*. Oxford: Oxford University Press, 1968.

Kelber, Werner. *The Oral and the Written Gospel: The Hermeneutics of Speaking and Writing in the Synoptic Tradition: Mark, Paul and Q*. Philadelphia: Fortress Press, 1984.

Kirschbaum, Engelbert. *Lexikon der Christlichen Ikonographie*. ("Art," "Bildnis" und "Evangelisten") Bd. 1. Rome: Herder, 1968. 301, 696ff.
See Leclercq.

Klinkenberg, Hans Martin. "Der Verfall des Quadriviums im frühen Mittelalter." *Studien und Texte zur Geistesgeschichte des Mittelalters* 5 (1959): 1-32.
See Riché.

Knowles, Dom David. *The Monastic Order in England. A History of Its Development from the Times of St. Dunstan to the Fourth Lateran Council, 943-1216*. Cambridge: Cambridge University Press, 1941.
See Riché.

Koep, Leo. *Das himmlische Buch in Antike und Christentum*. Bonn: P. Hanstein, 1952.
See Curtius.

Krafft, F. "Der Naturwissenschaftler und das Buch der Renaissance." In *Das Verhältnis der Humanisten zum Buch*, eds. F. Krafft and D. Wuttke, 23-41. Boppard: Boldt, 1977.
See Curtius.

Kretzenbacher, L. *Versoehnung im Jenseits. Zur Widerspiegelung des Apokatastasis-Denkens in Glaube, Hochdichtung und Legende*. Sitzungsbericht der Akademie. Munich: Verlagsbuchhandlung, 1971.
See Curtius.

Kuhn, Alvin. "Schriftsprache und Dialekt." *Cultura Neolatina* 16 (1956), fasc. 1: 35-51.

Ladner, Gerhart B. *The Idea of Reform: Its Impact on Christian Thought and Action in the Age of the Fathers*. Cambridge: Harvard University Press, 1959.

Lain Entralgo, Pedro. *The Therapy of the Word in Classical Antiquity.* New Haven: Yale University Press, 1970.

Lanza, Diego. *Lingua e discorso nell'Atene delle professioni.* Naples: Liguori, 1979.

Shows the slow penetration of documentation into the different circles of Athens during the fifth century.

Lares, Micheline-Maurice. "Types et optiques de traductions et adaptions de l'ancien Testament en Anglais du Haut Moyen Age." In *Bible and Medieval Culture*, ed. W. Lourdaux, 70ff. Leuven: Leuven University Press, 1979.

See Betz.

Leclercq, Jean. "Saint Bernhard et ses secrétaires." *Revue Benedectine* 61 (1951): 208-29.

Leclercq possesses an encyclopedic knowledge of the meaning given by twelfth-century monks to their gestures and words (*Otia* and *Vocabulaire*). On the habits of composing and dictating, see *L'amour*, especially pages 21ff. and 164ff., as well as De Ghellinck, *L'essort*, pp. 270ff. On the etymology of "dictation," see the linguist Ernout. Kirschbaum notices the transformation in the representation of Evangelists: from secretaries who listen to the voice of God frequently represented by a bird speaking in their ear, into secretaries copying from a scroll that descends from heaven. Dictation remained the only form of copying (Skeat) until word-division made silent copying possible (Saenger).

_____. *Étude sur le vocabulaire monastique du Moyen Age.* Rome: Herder, 1961.

_____. *L'amour des lettres et le désir de Dieu.* Paris: Aubier, 1963.

_____. *Otia monastica: étude sur le vocabulaire de la contemplation au moyen âge.* Freiburg: Herder, 1963.

_____. "Aspects spirituels de la symbolique du livre au XIIe siècle." In *L'homme devant Dieu II*, 63ff. Mélanges de Lubac. Paris: Aubier, 1964.

Lesky, A. "Homeros II: Oral Poetry; III: Mündlichkeit und Schriftlichkeit." In Pauy's *Realencyclopädie der classischen Alter-*

tumswissenschaft, ed. Wilhelm Kroll, 693-709. Supplementband XI, Stuttgart: 1968.

Lohmann, Johannes. "Verhältnis des abendländischen Menschen zur Sprache (Bewusstsein und unbewusste Form der Rede)." *Lexis* 3 (1953): 5-49.

The Greeks had no language, but only a way of life. Thought was embedded in the Logos. Classical science was critical but not yet judgmental. Truth still in the presence of Being. The two begin to separate only with Cicero: thought separates from language. However, the thinker remains argumentative; he does not become immediately judgmental. Only with nominalism does thought move away from language. It is only during the thirteenth century that language can be conceived of as a tool, an instrument that designates outside things. Rhetoric takes the place of logic. Modern language appears, a form for content. Language has changed from an organ of reflection into a sign of thought. Now with structuralism, the cycle is complete: language operates in persons.

Lord, Albert. "Homer, Parry and Huso." *American Journal of Archaeology* 53 (1948): 34-44.

————. *The Singer of Tales*. Cambridge: Harvard University Press, 1960.

————. "Perspectives on Recent Work on Oral Literature." In Duggan, *Oral Literature*, 1-24.

Luria, Aleksandr Romanovich. *Cognitive Development: Its Cultural and Social Foundations*. Cambridge: Harvard University Press, 1976.

Lynd, Helen Merrill. *On Shame and the Search for Identity*. New York: Science Editions, 1958.

Magoun, Francis Peabody. "The Oral Formulaic Character of Anglo-Saxon Narrative Poetry." *Speculum* 28 (1953): 446-67.

The first to apply Parry to *Beowulf*; challenged by Benson.

Manzaneres de Cirre, Manuela. *Arabistas españolas del siglo XIX*. Madrid: Instituto Hispano Arabe de Cultura, 1971.

Pages 7-15 provide a good introduction to the literature on Arabic translation in the thirteenth century.

Marrou, Henri Irenée. *A History of Education in Antiquity*. New York: Sheed and Ward, 1956.
See Riché.
_____. *Saint Augustin et la fin de la culture antique*. 4th ed. Paris: Ed. Boccard, 1958.

Augustine is not only the first major thinker who no longer writes in Greek, he is also the first whose entire philosophical formation was Latin. And it is a particular Latin, marked by the rhetoric of the late empire and its philosophers, full of enthusiastic diatribe, and technical artifices particularly attractive to the age. But his Latin remains in many ways the same kind of language for all antiquity: Reading is done out loud, and more often than not the author listens to a lector reading back to him what he has dictated. The scroll and the book—when it comes into existence—by their very nature prevent the reader from returning to a passage already read, and make scanning or leafing impossible.

During the sixth and seventh centuries, dialects have a strong influence on the written "Latin." Battisti and Wright oppose the often-voiced opinion "that Latin and Romance co-existed as spoken forms since Imperial times and were mutually unintelligible by the year 813" as untenable. Since the time of Augustine, the letters ceased to reflect the sounds—Väänänen. Menendez speaks of neo-Latin speech forms during the whole first millennium (pp. 1-5). Norberg explores its relations to the text of the Strasbourg Oaths. Pulgram speaks of the Council of Tours as a "resigned recognition that you cannot talk to people in a language that they have long ago ceased to speak nor thereby save their souls"—by the year 1000 the spoken Latin word had ceased to influence the orthography of Latin. Latin had become a historically quite unique language (Steiner and also Bischoff). Mohrmann gives an encyclopedic access to Latin's unique characteristics, and the history of its perception.

Martin, Henri-Jean, Roger Chartier, and Jean-Pierre Vivet. *Historie de l'édition française*. Tome I. *Le Livre conquérant du moyen âge au milieu du XVII siècle*. Paris: Promodis Français, 1984.

Many pages devoted to the manuscript, with many illustrations, which show the development of writing styles, binding, illustration, indices, and reference systems. Explores the changing role of the book in monastery, university, and in general culture. Also explores relations of lay piety to the book, written text, silent reading, and private study—all leading to individualism.

McKeon, Richard. "The Organization of Sciences and the Relation to Cultures in the Twelfth and Thirteenth Centuries." In *The Cultural Context of Learning and Thinking*, ed. Michael Cole, 151-92. New York: Basic Books, 1971.

McLuhan, Marshall. *The Gutenberg Galaxy: The Making of Typographic Man.* Toronto: Toronto University Press, 1962.

Meier, Christl. "Vergessen, Erinnern, Gedächtnis im Gott-Mensch Bezug: zu einem Grenzbereich der Allegorese bei Hildegard von Bingen und anderen Autoren des Mittelalters." In *Verbum et Signum*, ed. Hans Fromm, Wolfgang Harms, Uwe Ruberg, 143-94. Munich: W. Fink, 1975.
See Curtius.

————. "Zu Verhaeltnis von Text und Illustration bei Hildegard von Bingen." In *Hildegard von Bingen 1179-1979*, ed. A. Bruek, 159-69. Festschrift zum 800. Mainz: Todestag, 1979.
See Curtius.

————, ed. *Text und Bild. Aspekte des Zusammenwirkens Zweir Kuenste im Mittelalter und Frueher Neuzeite.* Wiesbaden: Reichert, 1980.

Menendez Pidal, Ramón. *Manual de gramática histórica española.* Madrid: Espasa-Calpe, 1958.

Mezey, Laszló, ed. *L'enseignement de l'écriture aux universités médiévales.* 2d ed. Budapest: Academie des Sciences de Hongrie, 1959.
See Riché.

Momigliano, A. "The Historians of the Classical World and Their Audiences." *Annali della Scuola Normale Superiore di Pisa* 8, no. 1 (1957): 59-75.
Underlines the dissynchronicity of cultural alphabetization. After Herodotus, historians quickly adopted mental conventions that devalued hearsay against documented evidence. But

the readers much more slowly asked for proof supporting those statements.

Morris, Collin. *The Discovery of the Individual 1050-1200*. The Church Historical Society. London: SPVC, 1972.

Without recourse to the apparatus of learned study, the author has mapped recent scholarship on the theme in an authoritative manner. He highlights (especially pp. 64-68) the relationship between various forms of self-description and the new style of self-perception. Chenu points with great competence to the decisive step in the discovery of the self (le sujet de soi-même) in Abelard: That intention determines the value of the act and therefore its sinfulness. The Church discipline demanding penance for the action had to be replaced by the confession of the evil intention: Each one had to learn to examine his own conscience, perceived as a book. Though the author is mainly concerned with the later fourteenth century, the historian Tentler documents the page-like perception of conscience. On the reflection of Individualism in literature, see Hanning and *Typus und Individualitaet*.

Müller, Gregor. *Die Wahrhaftigkeitspflicht und die Problematik der Lüge*. Freiburg: Herder, 1962.

See Fuhrmann.

Murphy, James J. *Medieval Rhetoric: A Select Bibliography*. Toronto: University of Toronto Press, 1971.

————. *Rhetoric in the Middle Ages: A History of Rhetorical Theory from St. Augustine to the Renaissance*. Berkeley: University of California Press, 1974.

Naveh, Joseph. *Early History of the Alphabet: An Introduction to West Semitic Epigraphy and Paleography*. Jerusalem: Hebrew University, 1982.

Nelson, H. L. W. "Die Latinisierungen in den Strassburger Eiden." *Vox Romanica* 25 (1966): 193-226.

New Literary History. Aspects of Orality: Vol. 8, no. 3 (1977). *Oral and Written Traditions in the Middle Ages*: Vol. 16, no. 1 (1984).

Nilgen, U. "Evangelisten." In Kirschbaum, *Lexikon*.

Nobis, H. M. "Die Umwandlung der mittelalterlichen Naturvorstellung. Ihre Ursachen and ihre Wissenschaftsgeschichten Folgen." *Archiv fuer Begriffsgeschichte* 13 (1960): 34-57.

Stresses the contrast between de-ciphering the Creator's handwriting in nature, and the de-scription of nature, which constitutes modern science. The metaphor is turned topsy-turvy in the transition from contemplation to description.

See Curtius.

Norberg, Dag. "A quelle époque a-t-on cessé de parler latin en Gaule?" *Annales Economies Sociétés Civilizations* 21 (1966): 346-55.

Notopoulos, James A. "Mnemosyne in Oral Literature." *Translations of the American Philosophical Association* 69 (1938): 465-93.

O'Connor, Michael Patrick. *Hebrew Verse Structure*. Winona Lake, Ind.: Eisenbrauns, 1980.

Oediger, F. W. *Über die Bildung der Geistlichen im späten Mittelalter.* Studien und Texte zur Geistesgeschichte des Mittelalters. Cologne: Brill, 1953.

See Riché.

Ohly, Friedrich. "Vom Sprichwort im Leben eines Dorfes." In *Volk, Sprache, Dichtung*, ed. Karl Bischoff and Lutz Röhrich, 276–93. Festgabe fuer Kurt Wagner, 1960.

Ohly's major intellectual influence lies in the field of medieval metaphor and semantics. In one exceptional paper ("Vom Sprichwort"), Ohly explicates the form and use of sayings as formulas in everyday village life—even today—and the delicate way in which variation from valley to valley contributes to the sense of local community.

Schmidt-Wiegand ("Rechtssprichwörter") examines the illustrations of legal proverbs in one of the earliest Germanic collections, and through her comments introduces the literature of the oral maxim. An attempt to classify the conversion of speech into equivalent sounds observed in many parts of the world is made by the linguist Stern. Ong's "Talking Drums" is interesting here. Taylor has made the proverb and its transmission into his life's work. While languages change, proverbs are often carried unchanged over centuries, as can be seen from a comparison of medieval sources with modern dialect-dictionaries (Berthold). This might be due to their formulaic character (Rothstein). They inspire artistic imagination, as Fraenger shows by analyzing a painting in which Peter Brueghel the Elder in 1559 has preserved about a dozen sayings that refer to the "world upside down." The Baroque use of sayings and proverbs in the creation of emblems, however, can be considered much more an "alphabetization" of these oral formulas than its interpretation. *InterDocumentation Company* now gives access to these. The riddle has a formulaic character that can be compared with that of the proverb and is part of every oral culture known (Taylor). Röhrich is an excellent critical introduction to the current state of "paroemiology"—the scientific study of proverbs. See there especially pages 75-77, an international bibliography on the study of legal maxims and their transmission.

————. "Das Buch der Natur bei Jean Paul." Studien zur Goethezeit. Erich Trunz zum 75. Geburtstag. *Beihefte zu Euphorion* 18, 177–232. Heidelberg, 1981.
See Curtius.

————. "Deus Geometra: Skizzen zur Geschichte einer Vorstellung von Gott." *Tradition als historische Kraft.* Festschrift Karl Hauk. Berlin, 1981.
Cassiodorus, *Institutiones* II, 5, 11: "geometra, quae est descriptio contemplativa formarum, documentum etiam visibile philosophorum."
See Curtius.

Ong, Walter J. *Ramus: Method, and the Decay of Dialogue.* Cambridge: Harvard University Press, 1958.

————. *The Presence of the Word.* New Haven and London: Yale University Press, 1967.

————. *Romance and Technology: Studies in the Interaction of Expression and Culture.* Ithaca and London: Cornell University Press, 1971.

A B C

————. "African Talking Drums and Oral Poetics." *New Literary History* 8, no. 3 (1972): 411-29.

————. "The Writer's Audience Is Always a Fiction." *Publications of the Modern Language Association* 90 (1975): 9-21.

————. *Interfaces of the Word*. Ithaca and London: Cornell University Press, 1977.

————. *Orality and Literacy: The Technologizing of the Word*. London: Methuen and Co., Ltd., 1982.
The best book on this subject.

————. "Reading, Technology and Human Consciousness." In *Literacy as a Human Problem*, Raymond, 17-201.

Paravicini, Werener, and Karl Ferdinand Werner, eds. *Histoire comparée de l'administration (4e-18 siècles). Actes du 14 colloque historique franco-allemand*. Beihefte der Francia Vol. 9. Munich: Artemis, 1980.
See Clanchy.

Parry, Adam, ed. *The Making of Homeric Verse: The Collected Papers of Milman Parry*. Oxford: The Clarendon Press, 1971.

Peabody, Berkley. *The Winged Word: A Study in the Technique of Ancient Greek Oral Composition as Seen Principally Through Hesiod's Works and Days*. Albany: State University of New York Press, 1975.

Percival, W. Keith. "The Applicability of Kuhn's Paradigm to the History of Linguistics." *Language* 52 (1976): 285-94.

Pinborg, Jan. *Die Entwicklung der Sprachtheorie im Mittelalter*. Beiträge zur Geschichte der Philosophie und Theologie des Mittelalters. Bd. 42, Heft 2. Aschendorff im Verbindung mit dem Verlag. Arne Frost-Hansen, Munster and Copenhagen, 1967.
See Borst.

Pörkesen, Uwe. *Der Erzähler im mittelhochdeutschen Epos. Formen seines Hervortretens bei Lamprecht, Konrad, Hartmann, in Worlframs Willehalm und in den "Spielmannseper."* Berlin: Schmidt, 1971.
"The medieval story-teller in many ways interrupts his story to tell us what he is doing: He gives a bird's-eye view of what he will be telling, tries to make people curious, insists on the importance of the subject he will deal with. He refers to authorities

that make him believable. Gets himself into the act. He is not afraid of preaching and being didactic. He praises his heroes, is sympathetic with them, berates them. . . . Nothing of the kind happens in the novel. To find a comparison we must turn today to a scientific paper. There the author tells us how important and unsolved the problem is, gives a summary, indicates connections, puts authorities into footnotes, thanks the teachers and colleagues . . ."

Pulgram, E. "Spoken and Written Latin." *Language* 26 (1950): 458-66.

Quinn, William A., and Audrey S. Hall. *Jongleur: A Modified Theory of Oral Improvisation and Its Effects on the Performance and Transmission of Middle English Romances*. Washington: University Press of America, 1982.

Rabinowitz, Isaak. "Word and Literature in Ancient Greece." *New Literary History* 4 (1974): 119-39.

Radding, Charles M. "Evolution of Medieval Mentalities: A Cognitive-Structural Approach." *The American Historical Review* 83 (1978): 577-97.
In the transition from government by custom to government by law (written) during the twelfth century, increasingly the intention of the self was taken into account: the *mens rea* became of interest to the judge.
See Watkins.

Rassow, P. "Die Kanzlei St. Bernhards von Clairvaux." *Studien und Mitteilungen zur Geschichte des Benediktiner-Ordens und seiner Zweige* 34 (1913): 63-103 and 243-93.
See Leclercq.

Rauch, Winthir. *Das Buch Gottes*. Munich: M. Hueber, 1961.
See Curtius.

Raymond, James C., ed. *Literacy as a Human Problem*. Mobile, Alabama: University of Alabama Press, 1982.

Redlich, Oswald. "Die Privaturkunden des Mittelalters." In *Urkundenlehre*, eds. Wilhelm Erben, L. Schmitz-Kallenberg, and O. Redlich. Munich and Berlin: Verlag Oldenbourg, 1911.
See Wattenbach.

Riché, Pierre. *Éducation et culture dans l'Occident barbare. 6. -8. siècles.* Paris: Editions du Seuil, 1962.

Encyclopedic orientation to the theme.

_____. *Écoles et enseignement dans le Haute Moyen Age.* Paris: Aubier, 1976.

_____. *Les écoles et l'enseignement dans l'Occident chrétien de la fin du 10 siècle au milieu du 11 siècle.* Paris: Aubier, 1979.

_____. "La Formation des scribes dans le monde merovingien et carolingien." In Paravicini and Werner, *Histoire*, 75-80.

_____. "Recherches sur l'instruction des laics du 9 au 12 siècle." In *Instruction et vie religieuse dans le Haut Moyen Age.* Section 10. Paris: Variorum Reprints, 1981.

Riché's work has become the standard handbook on education throughout the Middle Ages with reference also to elementary instruction in reading and writing—of course—mostly in Latin. For literacy among the Greeks, see F. D. Harvey. For the ideal of growing up, see the Classicist Jaeger (*Paideia*), and for the transformation of this ideal through growing literacy, see Marrou (*A History*) and Marrou (*Augustine*, the last chapter), in comparison with Jaeger (*Plato*). The latter two items introduce the transformation of early Classical Paideia into the Roman and then the Christian ideal of education. Best introduces the controversy about the spread of reading and writing abilities in Pompeii; see also Väänänen. Bischoff (*Schreibschule*) provides a detailed picture of elementary education in the Carolingian period in one area: Southeast Germany. See also in this same context Riché (*La Formation des scribes*). Bonaventura has some additional details on the method of teaching Latin, the only language in which writing was possible. Oediger gives easy access to texts relating to medieval clerical formation, and Glauche to the change in "textbooks."

Richter, Michael. "Latina Lingua—Sacra seu Vulgaris?" In *The Bible and Medieval Culture*, eds. W. Lourdaux and D. Verheles, 16-34. Leuven, 1979.

Deals with spoken Italian. See both Ewert and Steiner.

_____. *Sprache und Gesellschaft im Mittelalter: Untersuchungen zur mundlichen Kommunikation in England von der Mitte des elften bis zum Beginn des vierzehnten Jahrhunderts.* Monographien zur Geschichte des Mittelalters, Band 18. Stuttgart: Hiersmann, 1979. He argues that the attempt to reconstruct the spoken language cannot be left solely to philologists. As a historian, Richter attempts to sieve the sources for evidence of spoken language. See Steiner.

Röhrich, Lutz, and Wolfgang Mieder. *Sprichwort.* Sammlung Metzler Bd. 154. Realien zur Literatur, 1977. See Ohly.

Roncaglia, Martiniano. "I frati minori e lo studio della lingue orientali nel secolo 13." *Studi Francescani* 25 (1953): 169-84. See Steiner.

Rothacker, E. *Das "Buch" der Natur. Materialien und Grund sätzliches zur Metapherngeschichte. Aus dem Nachlass herausgegeben von Wilhelm Perpeet.* Bonn: Grundmann, 1979. See Curtius.

Rothstein, Robert A. "The Poetics of Proverbs." In *Studies Presented to Professor Roman Jakobson by His Students,* ed. Charles E. Gribble, 265-74. Cambridge: Slavica Publishers, 1968. Examines the formulaic character of sayings. See Ohly.

Rouse, Richard H. "The Early Library of the Sorbonne." *Scriptorium* 21 (1967): 42-71 and 227-52. See Daly.

Rouse, Richard H., and Mary A. Rouse. *Preachers, Florilegia and Sermons: Studies on the "Manipulus florum" of Thomas of Ireland.* Toronto: Toronto University Press, 1979. See Daly.

Ruberg, Uwe. "Mappae Mundi des Mittelalters im Zusammenwirken von Text und Bild." In C. Meier, *Text und Bild,* 550-92. 1980.

Russo, Joseph A. "A Closer Look at Homeric Formulas." *Transactions of the American Philosophical Association* 94 (1963): 235-47.

Saenger, Paul. "Silent Reading: Its Impact on Late Medieval Script and Society." *Viator* 13 (1982): 367-414. A brilliant summary with 274 footnotes leading to whatever is known about reading and writing activities, techniques and styles used, and the relationship of cultural history to the written page. Also useful to find representations of reading and writing activities during the period. For texts describing these activities, see Crosby and Scholz. Balogh very early argued that contemplative monks since the seventh century had tried to engage in the silent contemplation of pages. On the other hand, Chaytor (as McLuhan) holds to the idea that the invention of printing was the main factor that led to silent reading. The same idea is held from a Marxist point of view by Hajnal who marshals a rich array of sources. Some of the seeming contradictions might be due to the difficulty of defining what constitutes "silent" reading. Certainly silence was kept in the scriptorium of Cluny (Constable). Sign language was highly developed (Jarecki). For literature on the difference between composing and tracing the letters on the page, see Leclercq. Scholz analyzes vernacular literature, and not only in the Middle High German—of the twelfth and thirteenth centuries—but for all references to the *perception of a text*: read, hear, search, pick up, see. Believes that many texts were written for readers rather than listeners. The value of this work is its huge bibliographic coverage of the subject.

Schiller, A. Arthur. "Custom in Classical Roman Law." *Virginia Law Review* 24 (1938): 268-82.

A pithy introduction to the shifting meaning in Classical antiquity of the difference between custom/law; *nomos egraphos/nomos agraphos; mos-consuetudo/lex;* and so on.

See Watkins.

Schilling, Michael. *Imagines Mundi. Metaphorische Darstellung der Welt in der Emblematik.* Mikrokosmos 4. Frankfurt/Cirencester, England: Lang, 1979.

Deals with representations of the world as a book; especially pp. 71-81.

See Curtius.

Schmidt-Wiegand, Ruth. "Eid und Gelöbnis, Formel und Formular im mittelalterlichen Recht." In Classen, *Recht und Schrift.*

A thoroughly documented study on the transition from oral to recorded oaths. One of the several texts commented on is the oaths of Strasbourg; for these, see also Hilty, Nelson, and David.

_____. "Rechtssprichwörter und ihre Wiedergabe in dem Bild-handschriften des Sachsenspiegels." In C. Meier, *Text und Bild*, 593-629.
See Ohly.

Scholz, Manfred Gunter. *Horen und Lesen. Studien zur primaren Rezeption der Literatur im 12. und 13. Jahrhunderts.* Wiesbaden: Franz Steiner Verlag, 1980.

Schwarz, Alexander. "Die Bibel und die Grundlegung einer fränkischen Literatur." In *The Bible and Medieval Culture*, ed. W. Lourdaux and D. Verhelst. Mediaevalis Lovaniensia, Series I, Studia VII, 58-69. Leuven: Leuven University Press, 1979.
See Betz.

Sheehan, M. M. *The Will in Medieval England. From the Conversion of the Anglo-Saxons to the End of the Thirteenth Century.* Pontifical Institute of Mediaeval Studies and Texts, Vol. 6. Toronto, 1963.

Skeat, T. C. "The Use of Dictation in Ancient Book Production." *Proceedings of the British Academy* 42 (1956).
See Leclercq.

Spence, Jonathan D. *The Memory Palace of Matteo Ricci.* New York: Viking Penguin Publishers, Inc., 1984.
Matteo Ricci is a sixteenth-century Jesuit missionary who journeyed to China with ancient Greek memory systems—to aid Chinese in learning the Bible.

Steinberg, S. H. *Five Hundred Years of Printing.* 3d ed. Harmondsworth: Penguin, 1975.
See Steiner.

Steinen, W. von den. "Das mittelalterliche Latein als historisches Phaenomen." *Schweizer Zeitschrift für Geschichte* 7 (1957): 1-27.

Steiner, George. *Language and Silence: Essays on Language, Literature, and the Inhuman.* New York: Atheneum, 1970.

_____. *After Babel: Aspects of Language and Translation.* Oxford: Oxford University Press, 1977.

A B C

"List Saint Jerome, Luther, Dryden, Hölderlin, Novalis, Schleiermacher, Nietzsche, Ezra Pound, Valéry, MacKenna, Franz Rosenzweig, Walter Benjamin, Quine—and you have very nearly the sum total of those who have said anything fundamental or new about translation. The range of theoretic ideas, as distinct from the wealth of pragmatic notation, remains very small . . ."—*Babel*, p. 269. "Translation" presupposes two "languages": One of them, during the twelfth century, was always Latin. The majority of the population was ignorant of Latin, incapable of translating, but whoever learned Latin became a member of the European community (Grundmann, *Litteratus*). Literature translated from provençal into German was first turned into Latin, then into Mittelhochdeutsch (Pörkesen). During the twelfth century, new "languages" (that is, languages besides Hebrew, Greek, and Latin) move onto the horizon from several directions (Bischoff). German, for instance, "created" during the ninth and tenth centuries (see Borst) like Provençal, Catalan, and Italian, acquired the status of language.

Franciscans, during the first half of the thirteenth century, began to prepare missionaries for Islamic countries (Altaner, Manzaneres). Arabic was discovered as a language equivalent to Latin and Greek (Bossong). Finally, pilgrimage and crusade gave rise to the first guidebooks on elementary "language instructions." On the attempt to translate German customs in legal Latin, see Heck. On the Middle High German poet as "reteller," rather than translator, see Lofmark.

Stock, Brian. *The Implications of Literacy. Written Language and Models of Interpretation in the Eleventh and Twelfth Centuries.* Princeton: Princeton University Press, 1983.

Strauss, Leo. *Persecution and the Art of Writing.* Glencoe, Ill.: The Free Press, 1959.

Talbot, C. H. "The Universities and the Medieval Library." In *The English Library before 1700*, ed. Francis Wormald and C. E. Wright, 76-79. London: The Athlone Press, 1958.

Suggests that Friars were the force behind making books

smaller, since they needed to travel, and were also expected to be well read.
See Daly.

Taylor, Archer. *Selected Writings on Proverbs.* Ed. Wolfgang Mieder. Helsinki: Suomalainen Tiedeakatemia, 1975.
See Ohly.

Taylor, C. H., ed. *Anniversary Essays in Medieval History.* Boston and New York: Houghton Mifflin Company, 1929.
See especially Chapter One, "Libraries in the Twelfth Century: Their Catalogs and Contents."
See Daly.

Thompson, James Westfall. *The Literacy of the Laity in the Middle Ages.* University of California Publications in Education. Volume 9. New York: Burt Franklin, 1960.
See Grundmann.

Thomson, R. M. "The Library of Bury St. Edmunds in the Eleventh and Twelfth Centuries." *Speculum* 47 (1972): 617-45.
This library was built up—through gifts and purchases and by copying in the *scriptorium*—by one abbot, Anselm, between 1121 and 1148. By the end of the twelfth century, Bury contained bibles and liturgical books, texts of the main Church Fathers, pagan Latin classics, histories (Bede, Anglo-Saxon Chronicle), twelfth-century scholastic textbooks in divinity and law, and some "modern" Latin literature, such as the poems of Walter of Châtillon.
See Daly.

Typus und Individualitaet im Mittelalter. Report on a Conference About Middle-High German Literature. Munich: Fink, 1983.
See Morris.

Väänänen, Eva. *Le Latin vulgaire des Inscriptions Pompeiiennes.* Berlin: Auflage, 1966.

Vale, Malcolm Graham Allen. *Piety, Charity and Literacy Among the Yorkshire Gentry 1370-1480.* Borthwick Institute of Historical Research, Borthwick Papers number 50. York: St. Anthony's Press, 1976.

A B C

Veyne, Paul. *Les Grecs ont-ils cru à leurs mythes? Essai sur l'imagination constituante*. Paris: Du Sueil, 1983.

The author maintains that even today historians mainly tell not what is true, but what is interesting, or what they succeed in making sound so. Classical historians do not quote their sources, because they are convinced that they themselves constitute one. In a source, what happened and what could not but have happened fuse (p. 21) in the *Word* of the author. The author constitutes a mirror. He can neither lie nor be wrong.

Vinogradoff, Paul. "Customary Law." In *Legacy of the Middle Ages*, ed. C. G. Crump, 287-319. Oxford: Clarendon Press, 1927.

Men's conduct is regulated by two forces: by their habits of mind and by compulsion from outside authority—"laws" require generally a measure of support from the union and habit of people. . . . Charlemagne and other rulers were powerless so far as systematic legislation was concerned, although they left many traces in the form of particular institutions. Again in the twelfth and thirteenth centuries, writers on law explained that they had to deal mainly with customs and not with rules established by express legislation and embodied in an official code.

Medieval judges had to a great extent to discover the customary views and arrangements prevailing among the people; it became necessary to ascertain the nature and details of customs by applying for information to representatives or experts belonging to the community where the custom was in use. Judges settled disputes and rulers issued statutes in accordance with professional training, but their operations had to conform in one way or another to the customs of the folk.

See Watkins.

Vollrath, Hanna. "Gesetzgebung und Schriftlichkeit: Das Beispiel der angelsächsische Gesetze." *Historisches Jahrbuch* 99 (1979): 28-54.

Wang, Ching-Hsien. *Bell and Drum: A Study of Shi-Ching as Formulaic Language*. Berkeley: University of California Press, 1975.

Analysis of the formulaic content of pre-Confucian lyrical poetry.

The Alphabetization of the Popular Mind

Watkins, Calvert. "Studies in Indo-European Legal Language, Institutions and Mythology." *Indo-European and Indo-Europeans: Papers Presented at the Third Indo-European Conference at the University of Pennsylvania, 1966*. Ninth Publication in the Haney Foundation Series. Ed. by George Cardona, et al., 321-45. Philadelphia: University of Pennsylvania Press, 1968.

Legal texts are often among the earliest documents preserved. Their conservatism has been long recognized. However, the implications of this for the study of oral traditions has hardly been realized. Nuggets of "epic" formulation about customs are often carried unchanged through successive textual reformulation. Vinogradoff, long ago, pointed out that human conduct is regulated by two forces: habits and authority. In oral societies, habits can no more be separated from their perception as custom, than the rule they imply can be separated from the one-time concrete statement about it. A legislator like Charlemagne was powerless to shape behavior through statutes, even if he could leave some traces on particular institutions.

Even during what we here call the period of "intensive alphabetization"—during the twelfth and thirteenth centuries—writers on law explained that they had to deal mainly with customs. Judges settled disputes according to the law, but the reality conformed to nondescribable folk custom. During the twelfth century, folk customs were increasingly mis-represented as local "law" that was nonwritten. On the difference between unwritten law and custom, see Braybrooke and Diamond. Codification not only misread the nature of custom: retroactively, it "disembedded" the law.

Berman says, "There was a time prior to the late eleventh century when the peoples of Western Europe were not conscious of any clear distinction between legal institutions and other institutions of social coherence." The jurist is he who imputes this distinction to them: Schiller deals with this distinction in Roman law. The legal historian Michaud points out that the legal, written creation of an institution that results from a sworn pact among citizens (the corporation) of the twelfth century represents a significant step beyond the concept of a "moral person" present in the text of Ulpian quoted in Gratian's *Decretum*.

Classen is a source of valuable contributions on the impact of writing on the law of the Middle Ages.

Wattenbach, Wilhelm. *Das Schriftwesen im Mittelalter*. Leipzig: Auflage, 1896.

After four generations, this is still the reference manual for medieval script, as Bresslau and Redlich are on charters, and the much more recent Bischoff (1979) is on paleography.

Weinerich, H. "Typen der Gedaechtnismetaphorik." *Archiv fuer Begriffsgeschichte* (1964): 106-19.

Focuses on two key metaphors: The storage room and the Wax Tablet.

See Curtius.

Weissberger, L. "Ist Muttersprache eine germanische oder eine romantische Wortpraegung," *PBB* 62 (1938): 428-37.

Whitman, Cedric M. *Homer and the Homeric Tradition*. Cambridge: Harvard University Press, 1958.

"Geometric" structure of the *Iliad*.

Wolf, Ferdinand. *Über die Lais, Sequenzen und Leiche. Ein Beitrag zur Geschichte der Rythmischen Formen und Singweisen des Volksliedes und volksmassigen Kirchen und Kunstlieder im Mittelalter*. Original 1841. Reprinted Osnabruck: Zeller, 1965.

Wright, Roger. "Speaking, Reading and Writing Late Latin and Early Romance." *Neophilologus* 60, no. 17 (1976): 178-89.

Yates, Francis. *The Art of Memory*. London: Routledge and Kegan Paul, 1966.

The principal text on Ancient Mnemo-technical devices.

Zwettler, Michael J. *The Oral Tradition of Classical Arabic Poetry*. Columbus, Ohio: Ohio State University Press, 1977.

Index

A B C

alphabet *(cont.)*
  and creation of words, 7
  and creation of silence, 120
  effect on trust, power,
    possession and everyday
    status, 32
  in Greek curriculum, 23
  and Indian syllabary, 10
  introduction into
    England, 73
  invention of, 10
  techniques necessary for, x
  (see also North Semitic
    alphabet)
Aleph
  and absence of
    sound, 121
  and children of
    Israel, 121
  and Kabbalists, 121
amoeba words, xi, 106–07
Anglo-Saxon period, 22
ani, 72, 121
anthropologein, 3
aphona, 13
aphthonga, 13
Apollo, 14
St. Thomas Aquinas
  and concept of memory, 28
  and contingency, 91
  and lectures, 47
  and notes for memory
    aid, 48
  and *schemata,* 48
Arabic
  and the Hadramut, 8
  and the Koran, 63

Aristotle, 27
  and *anthropologein,* 3
  De Memoria et reminis-
    centia, 27
  and memory, 26
  and mimesis, 19
armas y letras, 66
  (*see* Nebrija)
Armenian language
  and "I," 124
ars dictaminis, 45
artificio, 69
  (*see* language and
    Nebrija)
Asia Minor, 12
Athena
  and duplicity, 85
a-tomos, 71
auctor
  and Chaucer, 91
auctoritas, 48
auctoritee, 91
St. Augustine
  City of God, 49
  The Confessions, 76–77, 83
  contemporary of Capella, 27
  and contingency, 91
  and *homo monolinguis,* 52
  On The Lie, 86–87
authentication, 42–43
author
  distinct from bards and
    storytellers, 87
  and fiction, 87
autobiography
  as American invention, 76
  and Benjamin Franklin, 73

A B C

Book of Life, 44
Book of Revelation, 59
Book of Self, 73
benedictions, 6
Borges, Jorge Luis, 54
Boswell, James, 73
brahmins, 6
Breca
  and Beowulf, 74
breve, 36, 37
brevicus, 49

C

Calendarium, 32
  (*see* Abbot Samson)
Campagne, 13
Cambrensis, Geraldus, 29
Canaan, 11
canon law
  and conscience, 85
The Canterbury Tales, 87–93
  and literacy, 88
  as literature, 90
  (*see* Chaucer)
Capella, Martianus
  *Marriage of Philology
    to Mercury*, 27
Carolingian
  handwriting, 60
  princes, 57
  reform, 58
  renovatio, 60

Carson, Rachel
  The Silent Spring, 118
Carver, George Washington
  and autobiography, 77
Casanova, Giovanni, 76
  and memoirs, 73
Cassiodorus, 49
caste
  Indian, 6
Castilian
  and grammar, 69
  as scriptural language, 69
catalogue, 39, 40
Caxton, William, 68
Cellini, Benvenuto
  and autobiography, 73
chancellory
  and copies of charters, 40
  and Strasbourg Oaths, 64
royal chancery, 36, 37
chants, 6
chapters
  and the Bible, 49
  and New Testament, 49
  and Old Testament, 49
Charlemagne, 55, 56
  and Alcuin, 60
  and language
    reform, 30, 58, 60
  and monks, 59
Charles the Bald, 56
charters
  and Book of Life, 44
  in common use, 36, 37
  and dating, 39, 41, 42
  and inheritance, 38

D

G

M

O

ABOUT THE AUTHORS

Ivan Illich's many books include *Deschooling Society* and *Gender*. Barry Sanders, Peter and Gloria Gold Professor of English and the History of Ideas at Pitzer College in Claremont, California, is coauthor with Paul Shepard of *The Sacred Paw: The Bear in Nature, Myth, and Literature*. His most recent book is *A Is for Ox: An Inquiry into Illiteracy and Contemporary Violence*.